Boston Boy

Boston Boy

growing up with jazz and other rebellious passions

by Nat Hentoff

PAUL DRY BOOKS

Philadelphia 2001

First Paul Dry Books Edition, 2001

Paul Dry Books, Inc.
Philadelphia, Pennsylvania
www.pauldrybooks.com

Text type: Linotype Sabon
Display type: ITC Eras
Designed by Adrianne Onderdonk Dudden
Composed by Duke & Company

1 3 5 7 9 8 6 4 2
Printed in the United States of America

Library of Congress Cataloging-in-Publication Data
Hentoff, Nat.
    Boston boy : growing up with jazz and other rebellious
passions / Nat Hentoff.
        p. cm.
    ISBN 0-9679675-2-X (pbk. : alk. paper)
        1. Hentoff, Nat — Childhood and youth. 2. Hentoff, Nat —
Homes and haunts — Massachusetts — Boston. 3. Authors,
American — 20th century — Biography. 4. Jews — Massachusetts —
Boston — Biography. 5. Music critics — United States — Biography.
6. Journalists — United States — Biography. 7. Boston (Mass.) —
Social life and customs. 8. Jazz — History and criticism.

PS3558.E575 Z464 2001
818'.5409 — dc21
[B]

                                                    2001051272
ISBN-13: 978-0-9679675-2-3

for Frances Sweeney

*Frances Sweeney, editor
of the* Boston City Reporter,
*for whom I reported on
anti-Semitism, and in all of
Boston, the woman I most
admired, sometimes feared,
and ridiculously loved.*

Long after the events described in *Boston Boy,* I was in the dressing room of Joe Williams, the longtime master of blues and ballads. We were talking about musicians whom we'd both known, dead before their time (whatever time that might have been). Suddenly, Joe looked at me and said, "You know, we're both survivors."

Joe was young when Jim Crow was old but still very hardy. And he'd lived the blues — in more ways than being black — before he became an international success. I didn't have to survive anywhere near so much, but I was pleased that Joe included me in that company. Later, thinking about what he'd said, I remembered that when I was not yet a teenager I had taken to such blues singers as Joe Turner and Bessie Smith because they were outsiders, as I was, a Jew in rampantly anti-Semitic Boston, all those years ago.

I've been an outsider since — by preference — having learned as a kid that you see a lot more about what's actually going on that way.

In *The Hub: Boston Past and Present,* Thomas O'Connor, the premier historian of my native city, mentions *Boston Boy,* referring to me "describing [my] travels from [my] home in Jewish Roxbury to the pleasures of Boston's black jazz scene." I was at home in those jazz clubs, more than I was in that other home. And this Boston boy, outsider as he was, wound up in Boston Latin School, founded in 1635, and began to learn enough so that he could go on to write this book.

Looking back at the roots of what I became, for better or worse, I am grateful, after all, to have been a Boston boy.

Nat Hentoff
New York 2001

Boston Boy

I would not have known I had been excommunicated had it not been for the news reports. The three rabbis, holding court in November 1982 at a motel in Tewksbury, Massachusetts, had blown mightily on a ram's horn and had then snuffed the candles, thereby extinguishing the spiritual lives of those once and former Jews on their list. The rabbis used as their text — the *Washington Post* reported — "the 1757 excommunication of a Jewish heretical group called the Satanic Sabbatian Frankists in Brode, Poland."

My link with the Satanic Sabbatian Frankists was my having signed a June 20 advertisement in the *New York Times* that year protesting Israel's invasion of Lebanon. I had therefore been charged by the rabbinical triumvirate of "collaboration with the enemy and committing a traitorous act."

Not for the first time, and not only by rabbis.

I only wished the three rabbis really had the authority to hold that court, that Bet Din. But rabbis these days have no power except over their own congregations, and that power can be removed, along with the rabbi, at the will of the congregation.

Ah, but had this been a true court, and had the rabbis believed that each Jew, however Satanic, must be given due process, they would have summoned me to that motel room, and I would have come. And I would have told them about my life as a heretic, a tradition I keep precisely because I am a Jew, and a tradition I was strengthened in because I came to know certain jazz musicians at so early an age that they, not unwittingly, were my chief rabbis for many years.

And in that motel room, I would be excommunicated nonetheless, for what could Duke Ellington and Charles Mingus mean to that court of assizes? But I would have been there, and I would have made my mark.

When the first Jews from Eastern Europe came, with their herrings and black bread, to Boston in 1882, they were told to go away. They were told this by the embarrassed German Jews of the city, who were afraid that the Brahmins might make some connection between these greenhorns and the true Jewish gentlemen and ladies of Boston. The first contingent of Eastern Europeans was thereupon shipped off to New York, which, God knows, would accept anything. But other Jews from Russia and Latvia and Hungary and Rumania and all those unfortunate places kept coming anyway, and stayed. Among them were Simon Hentoff (born in Wolkowysk, USSR, my FBI files tell me) and Lena Katzenberg (born, the FBI says, in Minsk, USSR — the FBI apparently considers Russia to have always been Bolshevik, for my parents left while the tsar still ruled).

I was their firstborn. As I learned quite soon, the German Jews were not the only Bostonians who wished that we Ostjuden had debarked elsewhere, far elsewhere. Senator Henry Cabot Lodge had proclaimed, without fear of political reprisal, that these immigrants and their progeny were "inferior." And Henry Brooks Adams, grandson of John Quincy Adams, had written of the "furtive Ysaac or Jacob still reeking of the Ghetto . . . snarling a weird Yiddish. . . . The Jew makes me creep."

It is no wonder, at least to me, that I was in my late teens before I dared go inside Brooks Brothers in Boston. The name, the look of the place, the look of the salespeople I saw through the window, all signaled that they would smell the ghetto on me and not make me welcome.

It was in this city — so admired by many who have never lived there — that I grew up. From the age of six, in a three-story apartment house on Howland Street in Roxbury. Once a neighboring town, Roxbury had been annexed by the city in 1867, and by the 1930s most of its churches had been transformed into synagogues. Its main shopping thoroughfare, Blue Hill Avenue, had such distinctive sights for tourists (had there been any) as an authentic herring man from the old country, standing stolidly but watchfully in the street next to a huge barrel of herrings. With his leather cap and bulky leather jacket, he was always there, sun and snow, early in the morning and in the twilight when it was time for me to hurry home to hear "Jack Armstrong, the All-American Boy" on the radio.

Tourists could also have seen small rabbis with very long beards, bristling boys swapping baseball cards, snapping them as if they were whips and then sliding the cards into their shirts as one of the small rabbis asked why they were not in cheder, in Hebrew school. Also visible on most days was a large, round, empty boy being wheeled about by his mother, who had warned him and warned him not to go out alone at night. And she had been so right — but she would never hear her sweet sixteen-year-old admit it, because he had been left in the gutter with an ice pick in his head. For what? What do you mean, for what? Nobody had to ask that question in my neighborhood.

My street, Howland Street, was not entirely Jewish. Toward the end of its four-block length were a number of black families. They had to walk past where we lived to catch the trolley car for Boston proper. We saw the same travelers every day, every month. But we never nodded or spoke to them, nor they to us. On our part of the street, they were referred to, not unkindly, as schwartzes. Not unkindly, because these schwartzes were clean, neat, and properly purposeful. But they *were* colored.

I lived on that street until I was nineteen, but only once was I allowed into one of the Negro homes. Through mutual friends across town, in a bohemian neighborhood of the Back Bay, I had gotten to know a fiercely intellectual Negro aesthete who seldom talked of race because he was training to be a universalist. And so he also seldom talked about himself. It was months before he told me he lived on Howland Street, and months more before he asked if I'd like to meet his great-grandfather. Born a slave nearly a hundred years before, the ancient man, I was told with an expectant smile, had read his way through whole libraries.

Small, startlingly thin, straight as a steel ruler, the former slave sat staring at me until I wondered desperately what I was supposed to say. Then, his tight bronze face still impassive, he said he knew I had gone to Boston Latin School and also had taken Greek. Accordingly, he asked my views on Homer, saying what a great pleasure it must be to read him in the original. Not having found it any sort of pleasure, because Greek had been taught like math at Boston Latin School, I mumbled my memory of exaltation.

After a while, emboldened by not having made a complete fool of myself (or so I thought), I asked *him* some questions. He was so old that surely he must have known, or heard stories about, the grand masters of Negro music: King Oliver, Duke Ellington, and way, way back, maybe, just maybe, Buddy Bolden. Could it be possible—why not? —that he might have actually heard that New Orleans cornettist-barber who went mad before there was anything to record him on?

The ancient man, without moving, flicked my questions away. And me as well.

"It's not your fault," the great-grandson said outside, "but I think he was kind of insulted. As if the only music he'd know anything about would be jazz."

"Does he know anything about jazz?"

The great-grandson smiled. "He'd never admit it if he did."

A tall, burly, dark-haired man with a riverboat gambler's long, flowing moustache, he keeps the windows of his first-floor apartment open all year long, except during blizzards and the more aggressive rainstorms. Music jumps through those windows as soon as he is up in the morning and until he leaves for work — "The Mooche," "East St. Louis Toodle-Oo," "Potato Head Blues," "Sent for You Yesterday, But Here You Come Today." Dark, growling trumpets; glistening cornets; smearing, mocking trombones; deep-blue clarinets — wickedly brash schwartze sounds to inflict on this Jewish block at the end of Howland Street hour after hour.

The riverboat gambler often sees me standing outside his window. On the street he is brusque, because he is always late to work. And I see him at no other time because he comes home at all hours of the night, as my mother says. But how does she know?

In time, as I begin to collect records myself, I learn to recognize most of the soloists streaming out of his window: Louis Armstrong, Bix Beiderbecke, Cootie Williams, Tricky Sam Nanton. And him, the dark-haired white man. Taking out his trombone, he often plays along with the records. His swaggering improvising is accented — the cadences are Yiddish — but it fits. Even when he sounds like he's bringing the circus to town.

When he left the house, swinging his trombone case, I'd wonder where he went to. Nobody in the neighborhood seemed to know. But I found out. Cutting classes at Boston Latin School one Monday morning, several friends and I race to the Old Howard on Scollay Square, Boston's — indeed, New England's — premier burlesque house. We have come to see Georgia Southern twist, glare, bump, and bite the air; and as we stare with mounting lust, I am insidiously distracted by a most familiar serenade — Tricky Sam Nanton's solo on "The Mooche." I look into the pit and there, playing that swivel-hipped solo, is my jazz-crazy neighbor, who winks at me.

Eating a huge salami sandwich very slowly, I sit in the middle of the morning on our porch, which overlooks Warren Street, around the corner from Howland. Warren Street is the main route to our shul, our synagogue, a block away. It is Yom Kippur, the Day of Atonement, the day of fasting, the day on which God marks down the fate of every Jew for the year ahead. Some of the Jews who look up at the slovenly, munching boy on the porch shake their heads in disgust. I stare at them, taking another bite. One old man, with a white beard almost as long as our rabbi's, shakes his fist at me. Another old man spits.

This despicable twelve-year-old atheist is waiting to be stoned. Hoping to be stoned. But not hit. I am, you see, protesting a stoning, or so I will say later that day when my father has discovered how his only son has spent the morning of the holiest day of the year disgracing himself and his father. By then, I am sick. Because of the sandwich. Because of the look on my father's face. But I will not say so. My father also does not speak, for if he did, he would disown me. My mother? I do not remember my mother having been there, but, of course, she was. She was never anywhere else.

A few weeks before, a young, handsome, smiling butcher had opened a shop two blocks away at Grove Hall, the secular center of our neighborhood: a drugstore, a bakery, a liquor store, a bank, a grocery, and Segal's Cafeteria, where most of the men for blocks around stopped on the way to work for a glass of tea and a bagel. For the taste of the food and the warmth of the companionship, there was no comparison between Segal's and the kitchens at home. So as not to offend their wives, some of the men had two breakfasts every morning, neglecting to tell their wives about the second.

The new butcher shop was five doors from Segal's Cafeteria, and three doors from the butcher shop that had always been in Grove Hall—the butcher shop where I had gone with my mother and my bubba, my grandmother, to watch the chickens being plucked and to peek at the butcher's two golden daughters, one of whom looked just like Priscilla Lane in the movies and paid me just as much attention.

Why did we need a new butcher shop? To have a choice, the signs on the new glass in the windows told us. A place where we could buy *both* kosher and nonkosher products. The Enlightenment was coming to Grove Hall. But a miscalculation had been made. The newcomer had somehow not found out that while we had five synagogues in the neighborhood, all five were Orthodox. This smiling butcher was actually going to sell trayf, unclean food, alongside kosher meat.

Oh, the signs in the windows and the leaflets pushed into our mailboxes assured us that the kosher and nonkosher meats would be rigorously separated in the new shop. This was the American way. The store would not take sides between religious and the nonreligious customers. Let each be served, and whatever the choice, the quality of the meat would be unmatched.

The night before the grand Monday opening, one of the

two windows in the new butcher shop was broken. Not just cracked, or with a small, cautious hole in it — there was no glass left at all, except on the sidewalk and in the store beneath what was once the window. The next day, with boards where the window had been, the door opened at eight. There were customers — bold women, the wives and daughters of Communists, Trotskyites, anarchists, and unadorned atheists in the community. *They* were known traitors, self-hating Jews. But on the sidewalk in front of the shop, old men and yeshiva students kept watch for newly revealed subversives. There were none. My mother, who was attracted to any new shop, "just to see what everything costs," peeked in the one intact window and decided she would come back when all the fuss was over.

The new butcher, still smiling, for he knew he could not be intimidated, guaranteed a glazier from outside the neighborhood a week's pay if he stayed by the shop for a couple of days. He was to start the next morning. On the night of the opening, the boards were neatly removed from the space left by the demolished window, and the other window was totally shattered.

By the end of the second day, both windows were newly vulnerable, and the butcher put up a handwritten sign reminding us all that we were in America, that he was an American citizen, as were his customers, and that everyone of us was entitled to life, liberty, the pursuit of happiness, and to our own choice in meats or anything else. That night, the windows disappeared again. The store was closed the next day, and the following morning a sign appeared announcing that it would reopen, under new management, as a kosher-only butcher shop.

I hadn't liked the butcher who had been driven out of Grove Hall. Too much smiling. But I was sorry that he was gone. Sorry and ashamed. Still, it wasn't true that my eating the salami sandwich in the open on Yom Kippur had been a protest against the smashing of the butcher's allegedly inalienable rights. I mainly wanted to know if I could do it, if I could stay on that porch until I finished that awful sandwich. I wanted to know how it felt to be an outcast. Except for my father's reaction and for getting sick, it turned out to be quite enjoyable.

Boston Latin School from eight in the morning until three in the afternoon. Among the alumni: Cotton Mather, Sam Adams, Charles Sumner, Ralph Waldo Emerson, Francis James Child (the collector of the Child Ballads), George Santayana, John F. ("Honey Fitz") Fitzgerald (grandfather of Jack Kennedy), Joseph P. Kennedy (father of Jack Kennedy), Bernard Berenson. And way up high, carved into the walls of the assembly hall, were other resounding names of those who had preceded me from 1635 on. What would the herring man have made of all this? In the extreme improbability of his ever going so far from Blue Hill Avenue as to come through these formidable doors across town on Avenue Louis Pasteur, the masters and the students would have laughed at him. Up their sleeves, of course, since they were gentlemen. And would

I have gone up to him, and welcomed him, and reminded him of the free pickles he used to give me when I had never even heard of the Boston Latin School? Fortunately the herring man never left his place beside his barrel.

I would not have been at Latin School to speculate on such matters had it not been for Miss Fitzgerald, my sixth-grade teacher at the William Lloyd Garrison School, where nearly all the students were Jewish and nearly all the teachers were Irish. Miss Fitzgerald expected everyone to learn exactly what had to be learned in her classes, and without excuses. Oh, she might have taken a heart attack into account, but children did not have heart attacks. She allowed no nonsense in the classroom — and everything not directly pertaining to the subject at hand was manifestly nonsense. She thought the most useful way to deal with the tender sensibilities of the young was to toughen those sensibilities. She snapped, she roared, she pounded her desk, and she froze miscreants of all sorts and sizes with the coldest eye I have ever seen. (Years later, musicians would describe, and I sometimes myself saw, Benny Goodman directing his Medusa eye — "The Ray" — at a fumbling sideman. There was nothing else like it in all of jazz. But in a faceoff, Miss Fitzgerald, without the slightest exertion, would have instantly turned Benny into stone.)

One afternoon Miss Fitzgerald marched from the William Lloyd Garrison School, all the long way down Elm Hill Avenue, turned into Howland Street, and proceeded to knock firmly on the door of our apartment. Accepting a glass of the usual scalding tea, which she polished off without a blink, Miss Fitzgerald told — actually, commanded — my mother to allow me to take the entrance examinations for Boston Latin School. If I applied myself, Miss Fitzgerald glared at me, I could do the work. And unlike the local high school, or, for that matter, all the other secondary schools in the city, Boston Latin School led to sure success in later life. Success for those — she glared at me again — who had the stick-to-it-iveness to stay the course.

Abruptly, she thanked my mother for the tea and commended her for letting me try to get into Boston Latin School. My mother had not said any such thing specifically, but her somewhat bewildered nod had been enough, for Miss Fitzgerald could not imagine any immigrant parent holding a child back from so bounding a head start on the ladder that might one day reach to the names carved high on the walls of the assembly hall on Avenue Louis Pasteur. That night, my father, of course, agreed. No one had asked *me*, but I would never have thought of crossing Miss Fitzgerald. Besides, as I knew quite well, even at ten, this was the way to penetrate the great mystery of my life. I would be going to *their* school, in *their* part of town, and so I would be not only learning Latin and Greek but learning about *them*.

After the seven hours at Latin School every weekday, there were two more hours in Hebrew school, plus three more hours on Sunday mornings. Both schools, of course, were generous in homework assignments. On Saturday evenings, moreover, I traveled a long way by trolley car for an hour's clarinet lesson with a tall, bony Scot in his seventies, who was retired from the Boston Symphony Orchestra. After our second year together, he told me that if I continued to apply myself, I might be able, in ten or fifteen years, to audition for the Boston Symphony with some expectation of being asked to try again.

I looked at the chocolate bars in my clarinet case and mumbled my appreciation of his dim fantasy. Actually, I very much liked the physical pleasures of playing — particularly the discovery that my fingers could be so quick and accurate. After all the *thinking* in English and Hebrew, the sensuousness of making music was so much fun that I was amazed I was allowed to have a musical instrument. But I did not find a lifetime of playing other people's music an inviting prospect.

If I had ever told that to the Scot, I could not have come back. We would both have been awkwardly conscious of my casual dismissal of his life. But I didn't want to leave, so I was plied with more exercises and pieces and canny fingerings in preparation for my distant ordeal at the Boston Symphony.

The Scot's wife was worried by the look of their Saturday visitor. She thought I needed more sleep, more games with the other lads in my neighborhood. What was I to tell her? What could I tell her? That I was a Jewish child, with immense responsibilities, and that these clarinet lessons were my only relaxation? Instead, I thanked her for her concern. And I meant it.

On the afternoon of the day in which I had sat eating a sandwich in plain view of throngs of Jews going to the synagogue for the Yom Kippur services, I went to shul too. First because, though quaking, I ached to be publicly denounced. My defiance would have been incomplete otherwise. It would have been silly, frivolous, without an echo. Like a tree falling without a sound in the forest.

I put on a suit and a white shirt and a dark tie and a yarmulke. On the way there, and among the people coming in and out, no one takes any notice of me, except for a couple of other dark boys who smirk as I pass by. In a separate swarm outside the shul, still other dark boys hit each other on the wrist with tightly knotted handkerchiefs. No one knows where this game started; it has long been part of the tradition of the High Holidays, at least among boys in all the synagogues of Boston. The object of the game is to inflict maximum pain with the stinging handkerchiefs, but without drawing any blood. He who cannot control his cruelty and *does* draw blood can in turn be made to bleed without constraint — except insofar as a knotted handkerchief is its own constraint.

I am asked to partake of these late-afternoon pleasures, but I move on. Inside, the fathers, and some sons beside them, are davening, praying, rocking back and forth, chanting, a swaying mass of sighs, the words of the prayers passionately blurred as they rise in the air, for each Jew sounds his own sacred rhythms. But instead of confusion, the prayers intertwine the same unmistakable meaning: let Jews finally be allowed to breathe without apology. And after a time, it is as if there were only one huge being in that room, a giant Jew made up of many shaking heads, each an insistent part of the whole.

I find my father, who, without a break in his chanting, opens a prayer book beside him and points to where everyone else is. I try — for once I really try — to follow the words rather than fake it. But I am seized with a compulsion to dare G-d, who must be here if He is anywhere on this day, to strike me dead if He exists. Here I am, I say inside my head, on the Day of Atonement in a shul, and I do not believe in you. Show yourself. Destroy me. But the davening went sighingly on, and I greatly resented His indifference.

The chazzan, the chazzan has come! A heavy man in his late fifties, with thick glasses and a face made for a cigar, he looks, on the street, like the grocer's assistant who will never have his own store. But now, in his black robes and high black skullcap, he looms over the congregation, and I stop snapping at God, for I am transfixed.

The chazzan closes his eyes as the spirit comes. What he sings is partly written, largely improvised. He is a master of melisma — for each sacred syllable there are three, four, six notes that climb and entwine, throbbing in wait for the next spiraling cluster. The chazzan is a tenor, what they call in opera a dramatic tenor, but what drama in opera is comparable to this continual dialogue with God? This is not an aria; there are consequences for those who speak to Him with false notes.

The voice is bold and clear, dark in color, but there is no heaviness. The chazzan soars effortlessly, pleading, demanding, refusing to allow God to forget for one moment that the Jews in this place have not forgotten *Him*, certainly not on this day, nor will they in all the days to come, so enough already! Or at least no more afflictions than last year. In the balcony, the women nod, and some moan, in agreement.

The cry. The krechts (a catch in the voice, a sob, a cry summoning centuries of ghosts of Jews). The dynamics of the chazzan are stunning — a thunderstorm of fierce yearning that reverberates throughout the shul. And then, as if the universe had lost a beat, there is sudden silence — but no, there *is* a sound, a far distant sound, coming, my God, from deep inside the chazzan, an intimation of falsetto, a sadness so unbearably compressed that I wonder the chazzan does not explode. The room is swaying; the chazzan, eyes still closed, does explode—his soul, riding a triumphant vibrato, goes right through the roof.

Years later, at a bar, between sets of the volcanic Charles Mingus Jazz Workshop, I am telling a black nationalist and Mingus about Jewish blues, blues that are thousands of years old, blues with plenty of their own soul. Mingus is interested. He wants to hear some. But the other guy, he says blues are only one color, his. Mingus says words sure do get in the way of hearing.

There is no one else on Elm Hill Avenue. It's too cold. But my exhilaration blocks out the cold. There, in my hand, is "I Wish I Could Shimmy Like My Sister Kate," the newest Muggsy Spanier Ragtimers record, on Bluebird, and in five minutes I'll be able to put it on my turntable at home. Rushing, I slip on the ice and fall hard. Frantic, I look at the recording still in my hand; but somehow it has survived.

"Hurt yourself, kid?" Standing in a semicircle above me are eight Irishers, about fifteen, sixteen years old. They are smiling.

"No, I'm okay." I decide to stay down for a while. I get the feeling that if I stand up, I'll be right down again.

"Break the record, kid?" the same solicitous goy — a strapping fellow, as they used to say — asks me.

"No. I was lucky." My smile is that of a mongoloid.

"You Jewish, kid?" There was no change in the tone. Just a friendly question. Before the execution.

I look up, indignant. "What do you mean, Jewish? I'm Greek. I don't live *here*. I just finished work."

"Where, kid? Where do you work?"

"Grove Hall. The drug store. Go ask him."

The leader of the Hibernians looks down at me, trying to remember if he's ever seen a Greek.

"He's a Hebe!" one of his companions snorts.

"Kid," the strapping boy stands over me, "say something in Greek."

If I could give Mr. Winslow, teacher of Greek at Boston Latin School, eternal life, I would do so right now. The Irisher didn't say it had to be *modern* Greek, so I begin the *Odyssey* for him. Naturally he says, "That's Greek to me," guffaws, and leaves me on the ground.

I stay there a while longer, on the theory that if I walk as fast as I know I will no matter how slow my head tells me to go, they will chase me. At last I pick up Muggsy Spanier, and all the way home I yearn to find on my path a fully loaded machine gun.

Every Sunday my two girl cousins and I, and our parents, would go for an afternoon ride. Often to the Blue Hills to buy fruit, or to other places where the children could get enough fresh air to last us through the week. On the way to the fresh air, we would pass churches, lots of churches. And each time, my cousins and I would spit out the window. It was as natural as breathing. Nobody had ever told us to acknowledge Christian houses of worship that way, but I couldn't remember when I hadn't spit at churches.

The grown-ups in the car never said a word, thereby giving their approval. Some years later, I was talking to an elderly aunt in Boston about the Sunday spitting. "Oh," she said, matter-of-factly, "we used to do it all the time in the old country. Not so they'd see us, of course."

Wherever we were on those Sunday rides, my father would stop the car by the side of the road just before three o'clock. Not only to better hear Father Charles E. Coughlin, parish priest of the Shrine of the Little Flower in Royal Oak, Michigan, on the radio. But also to keep us from crashing, because my father seriously doubted that he would have been able to control the car all the way through the good father's broadcast.

By the mid-1930s Coughlin, preaching every week against the bankers and other insatiable accumulators of wealth who were so painfully squeezing decent ordinary Americans, was much more popular than most elected leaders. Heard on thirty stations, he reached as many as forty million listeners, in addition to us by the roadside. As Alan Brinkley notes in *Voices of Protest: Huey Long, Father Coughlin, and the Great Depression,* "In Brockton, Massachusetts, referees halted schoolboy football games shortly before three o'clock on Sunday afternoons so that parents, coaches, and players could get to a radio in time to hear Father Coughlin. When the sermons were over, the games resumed. In churches around the country, pastors rescheduled Sunday services so they would not conflict with the radio discourses."

And when this seductive priest came himself to the cities, "in Cincinnati, Chicago, Boston, Baltimore, and St. Louis, adoring crowds packed stadiums and auditoriums to hear him or lined his route to and from the train stations just to glimpse him passing by." Ah, but Boston revered him most of all. James Michael Curley, our grandly lyrical mayor, also a devout believer in sharing the wealth, declared Boston to be the "strongest Coughlin city in America."

The priest, though born in Ontario, had just the lightest touch of a brogue. An appealing, flowing voice, and though capable of icy wrath at Communists and Fascists and, of course, bankers, it could also sing liltingly in your ear of the new day coming when real Americans would be running this country again. (No wonder he had to hire 145 people to answer his mail.)

By the mid-1930s, previous intimations of anti-Semitism in Coughlin — so fleeting and veiled that even many Jews had not quite believed what they heard — had become the real thing, as unmistakable as a punch in the nose. The international bankers and the international Communists were somehow one and the same. Jews. And all other Jews were suspect, for were not Jews all of a clan? I still remember hearing on a crisp October Sunday that gently indignant voice tolling the names of the members of the Politburo. After nearly every name, a pause, and then the good father would add, like a blow, " — A Jew!" In the car, we all knew better. We all knew who was a Jew and who was not. And this priest, who surely did not move his lips when he read, also must know. So why was he lying? We knew why.

He had a newspaper, this priest. *Social Justice*. It was

sold on Sundays, before each mass, at the Catholic churches in Boston and everywhere else. Those who wrote for *Social Justice* were fascinated by Jews, for we were in practically every issue. It was in *Social Justice* that I first learned of "The Protocols of the Elders of Zion" — a ceaseless Jewish conspiracy to take over the world. The whole world. *Social Justice* was read in the Catholic parlors of Boston on Sunday afternoons, chewed over at the dinner table that night and Monday night as well, until by Tuesday the gracious sons of those households, their knuckles itching to celebrate the glory of Christ, were sufficiently inspired to go forth again among the Jews and break their heads.

In our car, there was silence as the priest from the Shrine of the Little Flower spoke. Each of us needed to hear every word. The adults in the car had heard similar words, though not nearly so lyrically phrased, and the words had become pogroms. My mother, when a very little girl, was popped into the cold oven by her mother just before the dashing Cossacks smashed in the door. My bubba didn't think they'd stay to eat.

And my cousins and I, citizens of this New World by birth, listened just as intently to Father Coughlin. We felt hunted too. None of us had the slightest doubt, on those Sunday afternoons, that pogroms could happen here too. The silence among us continued for quite a while after the priest had gone. In the late afternoon, to complete the day of rest, we heard William Shirer from Hitler's Berlin. But at night there were Jack Benny with Rochester, Dennis Day, and Don Wilson, and all the shows after, and we children forgot Father Coughlin. Until just before we went to sleep.

Some afternoons, especially in the spring, the invitation to play baseball-against-the-stairs or hit-the-ball in the middle of the street was so alluring that I never showed up at the Hebrew school on Elm Hill Avenue. My absence was not mourned. Continually angry at being forced to attend *two* schools, one of them the hardest in the city and probably in the country, I was beloved by no one in the other school, the school of my ancestors. I dunked girls' braids into inkwells, threw spitballs (this was America, was it not?), and coolly withheld respect from the ardent, underpaid teachers.

Yet, despite the mutual pleasure caused by my absence, I didn't skip Hebrew school often. It wasn't worth the trouble. Part of the trouble was my father, who insisted I stay until I was bar mitzvahed, and since he rarely insisted on anything, I took him seriously when he did. The alternative was weeks of his cold silence, and anything was preferable to that. Indeed, there was much prolonged silence in our home, for both my mother and my father often placed each other in Coventry. In an apartment of two small bedrooms, a small living room, and a narrow kitchen, colliding silences over a long period of time can create much anxiety, especially in a noncombatant.

The other problem in skipping the second round of schooling for the day was the little rebbe. With his white beard reaching almost to his knees, he could play a congregation like Nathan Milstein. And on the street, one on one with a boy, it didn't matter how much taller the boy was than he, the rebbe was a commanding presence.

About to bang the rubber ball against the stairs, I would feel the rabbinical presence and, turning, be slapped with a question that was not a question. "Nosson, you are not in cheder today?" The ball in my hand, I confessed I was not and said the doctor had told my mother I must have more fresh air. Or I said I had a cold and did not want to infect my classmates in cheder. (Of course, my answer implied, it didn't matter if the heathen in the street were exposed and caught pneumonia.)

Whatever the lie, the rebbe ignored it, wagged a surprisingly long finger at me, and said, "The bar mitzvah is coming, Nosson, the bar mitzvah is coming."

One evening, three friends and I are walking through large, dark Franklin Park on the way to a dance at the Hebrew school. Coming toward us are four bigger boys. When they are close enough, it is clear they are not Jewish. And since they are not Italian, they are Irish. Their leader swaggers up to me and asks — what else? — "Are you Jewish?" Since there are other members of my tribe with me, my Greek option is gone. I nod.

"You got a light?" he asks.

As I go to my pocket, I look down, and a stone, a huge stone, smashes into my face. Or so it feels. The shock and pain are such that it takes a few moments for me to taste the blood and feel the space where, a second ago, there had been a tooth. Their leader, rubbing his fist with satisfaction, waits for a revengeful lunge and is not surprised when it doesn't come. So few of these kikes fight back. He and his sturdy companions move on, guffawing.

By the time we get to the Hebrew school, the blood is all over my white shirt. The four of us, with genuine modesty, tell of how we forced our attackers to flee back where they came from, and we are the toast of the evening. We do not regret the lie. It is one thing to know that we of the Yiddishe kops will grow up to be served by these goyishe hooligans fattened into loutish laborers, garbage men, firemen, and cops. But we are not grown yet, and we see the same movies on Saturday that the hooligans do. And though we do not have to be convinced by our parents not to fight — because we know that some of our sisters can beat us up — we do not enjoy knowing we do not know how to put up our dukes. We are afraid to put up our dukes. We hate it.

Years later, as I was learning about active nonviolence from A. J. Muste, the radical pacifist who was the first to intrigue Martin Luther King with the possibilities of soul force, Muste told me a story. When he was eleven, in Grand Rapids, Michigan, the bully of the school had advanced on him. A.J. stood his ground, trying neither to defend himself physically nor to run away. Taken off guard, the bully hesitated, shifted his weight from one leg to the other, hitched one of his shoulders, and, followed by his bewildered claque, turned and walked away.

I told A.J. I found this inexplicable. That night in Franklin Park, I said, I hadn't tried to defend myself or to run. I had just stood there. So why hadn't soul force worked for me?

"It may be," said A.J., "that the difference was when that boy came toward me, I, for some unfathomable reason, no longer felt afraid or nervous, as I had up to that moment. And he knew I was not afraid. Therefore, I had no need of defense, and so I was safe. That was spiritual force, and it is just as real as physical power."

I could have hit A.J.

There may have been one or two Jewish boys in Roxbury who reached thirteen without being bar mitzvahed. An outside observer might have thought there'd be quite a few, because socialist, anarchist, Communist, and Trotskyite periodicals were not without eager readers in our neighborhood. Yet even *those* fathers, those vicarious revolutionaries, would have felt that *their* fathers would have been deprived and shamed if, after centuries, one of their seed should not publicly be received as a Jewish adult, "the son of the Commandment," on a Saturday in the synagogue.

For a boy not to go up to the Torah on that day and leave it a man meant that he had abandoned his people. In a ghetto, this was hard to do. As I say, there may have been one or two such Roxbury Jewish boys through the years, but I never heard of them.

My father arranged for one of the teachers in the Hebrew school to tutor me for the day of the bar mitzvah. Tutor me in the reading — and the *understanding* of the reading — from the Scroll of Law. And especially, as a boy who had never sung in public, or in private, for that matter, I was to be tutored in the chanting of the lesson from the Prophets that would fall at the time of my bar mitzvah. The speech at the end, my claiming of manhood, I would write myself, in Hebrew, but the tutor would perfect it.

Halfway through the tutoring, I was thrown out of

Hebrew school. My regular teacher in the school that year, a stiff, heavy man in his fifties, had two great passions — the Jewish people in general (myself excepted) and his wife. In class, he worked hard to rescue us from whatever falsehoods contradicting his teachings we might have been told in *their* schools earlier in the day. If any of us disputed him, he took that as disloyalty — to him personally, to the Torah, and to the Jewish people from before and during the Diaspora.

I disputed him regularly, it being inconceivable to me that this minor-league Hebrew school teacher — he wasn't even in a yeshiva teaching future rabbis! — could seriously challenge the masters of Boston Latin School. One late afternoon I went too far. I made fun of one of his alleged historical facts, and the class laughed.

"If you know so much," he shouted, "why are you here? Why do you go to cheder at all, Nosson?"

"For the bar mitzvah!" I yelled back. "Why *else* would I waste my time here?"

"*Out!*" He pointed to the door. "*Out!*" The fist he was making did not seem just rhetorical so I left.

One thing about this teacher — who ended my formal instruction in my heritage — puzzled me. And disturbed me. From the time I was a small boy, and indeed until I left the neighborhood some years later, I often saw him and his wife strolling, usually on Sundays. Hand in hand. Always hand in hand. She too was large but more gracefully shaped than he, and she seemed utterly fascinated by whatever he was saying. As he was when she spoke.

The sight was so strange in our neighborhood. A married couple of that age, or of any age for that matter, showing open affection for each other. But especially at that age! I envied him, but I couldn't understand how this man, whose fingers were intertwined with hers, could be the dusty curator of my cheder class too.

My father pleaded with my tutor to continue working with me even though his colleague had thrown me out of the school. The tutor agreed, and the bar mitzvah came. As the services began, I figured that if I could keep my concentration and appear self-assured, I'd be able to get to the end of the ritual without mortifying myself and my family. Then I looked up and saw, coming down the aisle, Rabbi Joseph Dov Soloveitchik. Tall, his posture almost military, his eyes piercing, he had a long black beard, the blackest beard I had ever seen or imagined. There was a rustle of recognition, for although the Polish-born Soloveitchik had been in Boston for only six years, he was already regarded as a formidable scholar and a powerful spiritual presence. (He has since become the leading force in modern Orthodoxy throughout the world.)

In those days Rabbi Soloveitchik, I later found out, frequently spent Saturday mornings in various synagogues to observe for himself what manner of new men were coming into Judaism. This morning, he sat down in the front row, and as I began to chant, the rabbi, in his deep, resonant voice, started chanting along with me.

"*If* you make a mistake," my tutor had told me, "don't go back. Only the Jews of the regular congregation will know you have made a mistake. The rest, the Jews who show up only for the holidays and bar mitzvahs, won't know the difference — *if* you do not show anything on your face, and *if* you do not stop and go back."

Now, I was thinking desperately, everybody will know every mistake I make, because Rabbi Soloveitchik's sonorously clear obbligato is making all too unmistakable every syllable I *should* be singing.

At the end, utterly spent, I finally dared to look directly at Rabbi Soloveitchik. I could read neither approval nor disapproval in his face, but as he nodded gravely to me, there was a slight smile. The Jewish people had survived my bar mitzvah.

I have not seen him since, but I follow Rabbi Soloveitchik and his works in the Jewish press. His focus, as a philosopher, is on loneliness and homelessness, and he rejects the notion that Orthodoxy must stay withdrawn from the rest of contemporary life. I was especially impressed when Rabbi Soloveitchik turned down the post of chief Ashkenazic rabbi of Israel. "I was afraid to be an officer of the state," he said. "A rabbinate linked up with the state cannot be entirely free." As for the personal power in Israel that he had thereby denied himself, the rabbi noted that the idea of exile is "the essence of the Jewish people."

So I felt as a child, and still do.

When in November 1982 I received the news of my alleged excommunication from the Jewish people by the three rabbis in the Tewksbury, Massachusetts, motel, my immediate fantasy was to call Rabbi Soloveitchik and ask if he would take my case. With his enormous authority, he could insist on a rehearing, this time including all necessary elements of due process. And then, with his scholarship and soul force, he would smite that tribunal into sawdust.

Indeed, had I been given any warning of those rites, I actually would have called Rabbi Soloveitchik, and I do believe he would have taken the case. Even though I had long long since abandoned our common G-d. But I had not abandoned our people, whatever *they* might think.

After that Saturday, I was not in a synagogue again, for religious purposes, for thirty-six years. I had gone to hear Israeli dissidents in shuls, and had attended other meetings that did not involve davening. But at last, a Saturday came when I had to read from the Torah again.

On this Saturday morning in 1974, an elderly member of the congregation was handing out the prayer books. It was a few minutes before the bar mitzvah of my elder son, Nicholas, would begin. Still spry, his hair more red than gray, my fellow Jew congratulated me in advance and then, shaking his head, took the tallis (the fringed prayer shawl) from my shoulders, reversed it, and placed it back on my shoulders.

"The text!" He looked at me sternly. "When you have a prayer shawl that has a text around the collar, the words must be seen! They are a benediction saying that you are wrapping yourself in this tallis as a badge of your Judaism." Frowning, he asked me, "You went to cheder?"

I nodded. "Until, or almost until, my bar mitzvah. Then I stopped."

"And shul—you stopped going to shul too?"

I nodded again.

"It happens," the nimble elderly man said. "When it is time to go into the other world, you have to make a decision whether you're going to be a Jewish fella—or you're not. It's a matter of choice. I chose to go in this direction"—he gestured in a gently proprietary manner toward the

Holy Ark, behind whose drawn curtains the Scrolls of the Torah were in place.

But since I had made the decision so long ago that I was not going to be his kind of Jewish fella, why was I here now? Or rather, why was my elder son here?

I'm still not entirely sure. Nick was never told he must be certified as a Jew. Oh, he knew he was Jewish, all right, but not from ever having gone to cheder or, as a member of a congregation, to shul. He knew he was Jewish because of conversations he heard at home, at relatives' homes, and at the annual Passover Seder, which, I would have thought, had about as much religious impact on him as a Marx Brothers movie, which it resembled.

My son's explanation is that he was seized with the utterly compelling need to be bar mitzvahed because we had taken him to see a Broadway musical, *The Rothschilds,* and later the movie version of *Fiddler on the Roof.* Why not? A vibrant, dancing tune can be just the right ticket to a pulsing sense of community. The Chasids know that.

Still, that morning, I was trying again to figure out why Nick had asked for, had demanded that he take on the burdens of becoming an official Jew. The Hebrew lessons. The lessons with the chazzan, the cantor, a Yugoslavian who had escaped from a concentration camp and had then gone on to work for the underground in Rome. He was a chazzan of intricate power and stunning subtlety. And he was a testy man whom God had mistaken for Job, having inflicted on him so many scatter-brained bar mitzvah boys in the new country.

"Sing!" the chazzan had commanded a tentative Nick during the rehearsals. "If you don't know, if you get stuck, open your mouth anyway. Listen to me! If you make a mistake, go on! Most of the people there won't know the difference. Open your mouth!"

I had just turned from the red-headed keeper of the prayer books when suddenly a voice, a voice in full cry, praying, rose from the back of the shul, and all conversation stopped. It was a procession, moving slowly but inexorably. At the head was the rabbi of the synagogue. Behind him were the cantor and the assistant rabbi, all three in black robes and black skullcaps. Between the cantor and the assistant rabbi, looking so small that he seemed to be not yet ripe enough to be bar mitzvahed, was Nick, with a white skullcap and a blue-and-white tallis, the text up, around his shoulders.

The kid came through. The reading from the Torah, the singing from the Prophets, the Haftorah. The high, clear voice reverberating through the centuries. All the years before, if anyone had asked, I would have said that it did not make a bit of difference to me if Nick was bar mitzvahed or not. I meant it. Until that morning, when I felt the ghosts of all those whose name, in one spelling or another, I bear, whispering with satisfaction that they had not been abandoned.

At the end, in his speech, Nick noted that "Jewish people have been badly treated in most cultures. Even in the United States, when some of the earlier Jewish immigrants got off the boat, they were treated like cattle. If the immigration officials couldn't pronounce their names, the inspectors would just brand them with a new name. The Jewish immigrants often lived in slums surrounded by people who did not like having them there.

"When my father was a child, living in a Jewish neighborhood, the Jewish kids were often preyed on by groups of Italian and Irish kids. Once, my father had to say he was a Greek or he would have gotten beat up. I think it is horrible that a boy who is proud of his religion should have to deny his religion under the threat of getting beaten up."

It was a singular experience, I found, trying to compose the proper facial expression while being celebrated as a coward. I wished that instead Nick had told another story of mine about the Jewish ghetto in Roxbury in those years.

Mickey Cohen was a rarity in our neighborhood. He was a professional boxer. A welterweight. We had fruit peddlers, grocers, traveling salesmen, dentists, garment workers, druggists, a doctor, house painters, barbers, bakers, delicatessen men but only this one actual, professional dealer in klops — blows. There were ambivalent feelings about a Jewish boy making a living with his fists, but most of the neighborhood took pride in Mickey because he was moving up. There had been talk among the prizefight crowd that the Yid might get a shot at the title. He was a hell of a boxer, you see, but who would have thought that a Yid could hit like that?

It was an evening in early fall, the year of my bar mitzvah, 1938. In Grove Hall, the lights had just gone on in the drugstore, in Segal's Cafeteria, the bakery, the kosher-only butcher shop, and the liquor store. When he was around, Mickey could usually be found leaning, leaning very lightly, against the window of the liquor store.

He was not a patron of the liquor store, for Mickey was always in training, but he liked the spot because it gave him a panoramic view of Grove Hall. Considering the unflagging interest he seemed to have in the details of our shtetl life, Mickey might have been our own version of a novelist in a small Southern town. But you'd never know from talking to him because he hardly ever spoke. Oh, he'd politely acknowledge everyone, from children to grandfathers, who wished him well in his next bout. ("It's gonna be a tough one," Mickey would nod. "That's for sure.") But most of the time he just leaned against the liquor store window and watched.

On that fall evening, careening out of a side street into Grove Hall came eight young men in their late teens and early twenties. "Irishers," a scholar in front of Segal's Cafeteria said as he scuttled inside. And so they were, strong-looking lads, smiling lads, as one snatched a yeshiva boy's glasses from his face and spun them into the street; as another dumped the newsboy's first batch of *Daily Records* into the gutter; as yet another high-spirited young man yanked, as he had seen in the newsreels, an old, spidery Jew by his beard.

By then they had come to the liquor store window and to Mickey, leaning against it. Mickey had not gone after any of them — he had not started it, everyone agreed when it was all over. So even if one of those lilting, wild colonial boys should stay hurt, or even — oh, who could even say the words? — should *die* as a result of what happened, why,

Mickey was not to blame. He had only been acting in self-defense.

And that was God's truth. Except afterwards, no one could be found who was able to detail the exact sequence of the horribly satisfying events. There was general agreement that two pairs of hands, bold Irish hands, had been stretched out, with a pair of Irish grins, to take Mickey by the legs and slide him off the liquor store window. But then — well, it was like one of those silent movies speeded up. A blur of leaps and fists and crashes, with the reel seeming simultaneously to be going forward and backward.

In a few minutes, it was over. The eight of them, the Irishers, all broken up. Five of the poor souls were on the sidewalk. One in the gutter, his head poking through a *Daily Record*, like a three-dimensional front page. Still another, ass up, lay in the doorway of the liquor shop. A third was splotched against the window. On their smashed faces were looks of the most awful astonishment, as if they were about to wake up in Transylvania. The two still awake were bent over, moaning, one of them throwing up and the other crying, in a child's voice, "My balls, you've kicked in my balls."

"Save you money, if I have," Mickey said matter-of-factly, kicking him once more, into his companion's vomit. "Kids cost an arm and a leg these days."

Mickey surveyed the rest of the battlefield, and as one of the collapsed invaders tried to get to his feet, Mickey stiff-armed him back down into a doorway, where he appeared content to lay docilely, staring at Mickey in what I do believe was a form of worship.

But how, how had this miracle happened? Eight of them,

eight of *them,* struck down by one of us. A very special one of us, to be sure, but still, only one. As best as we boys could reconstruct it, and we devoted hours and hours for years in the sweet attempt, when two of them started going for Mickey's legs, he gave his legs to the Irishers — one in the balls and the other in the stomach. The rest of the merry band came over on the double, of course, but they were simply unprepared for the swift and terrible precision of this Hebe's dance of destruction.

Worse yet, the Hebe completely ignored the Marquess of Queensberry rules to which he had sworn an oath — but you know how these Jews are about oaths. There were not only nose-crunching jabs and right crosses that removed all worry about cavities in a good many of their former front teeth, but there also rained upon these low-class Cossacks such knocks on the Adam's apple, such pounding of the kidneys, such banging of the balls, that it was a wonder they were all eventually able, in the merciful darkness, to drag themselves out of Grove Hall. Not looking back, not saying a word, their hearts full of home. Without expression, Mickey, his shoulders against the liquor store window, watched them go.

We, kids and adults, kept a certain distance from Mickey that night. Mostly in awe, but partly because, as much as we delighted, reveled, in the near dismemberment of our enemies, there was in us a touch, buried but there, of aversion to even *his* redemptive, glorious violence. Walking through Grove Hall, or at night on the edge of sleep, we replayed, in color, those scenes of carnage, but there was something illicit about the satisfaction we took in all that hitting, all that smashing of faces. It was — it was un-Jewish.

But that was long ago. We were, you must remember, ghetto Jews.

I remember them now as ugly books. All had the same cheap brown binding—an institutional color, like the paint in waiting rooms for jurors. There were no illustrations, and the print seemed to get dimmer with each reading.

But those were *my* books, bought at fifty cents a week —plus a coupon from the Hearst daily, the *Boston American*—out of my afterschool and weekend earnings. They were the classics! *The Autobiography of Benjamin Franklin, The Last of the Mohicans, Ivanhoe, Tom Sawyer,* and other hallmarks of a sophisticated library.

I was addicted to books. Both the reading of them and the physical possession of them. On the way home from Boston Latin School, I would sometimes stop at an astonishing building that had nothing but used books, four floors of them. And while hunting for jazz records in other parts of the city, I would often find some in the backrooms of bookshops. And every time my father took me for a ride to the railroad station to make the last mail connection to New York, it was understood that I would not return home without at least one new book. Soon the books burst out of my bedroom and took over nearly all the wall space in the front hall of our apartment as well as the living room.

A Latin School friend in those years was Daniel Yankelovich, who in time became a distinguished pollster and analyst of the auguries detected by his surveys. When we visited each other's homes, one of the main purposes was to count each other's books. The winner would crow over the insufficient intellectual.

Still, for all my lust to own books, all week long I made and remade lists of the books I would take out of the public library on Saturday morning. Our branch was a spacious series of rooms on the first floor of the huge Roxbury Memorial High School, ten blocks from where I lived. Although children were technically restricted to the children's section, the crisp Irish and Jewish librarians didn't care where we found our books so long as we behaved like gentlemen and ladies.

And so long as we did behave like mature readers, we were treated with no less consideration and patience than if we were adults. When, at eleven, I checked out a massive biography of Lenin, the librarian at the desk asked no questions, nor did she some weeks later when I borrowed Albert Schweitzer's *The Quest of the Historical Jesus*.

I did not ignore the children's section by any means, reading and rereading every one of Andrew Lang's Color Fairy Books — Red, Olive, Blue, Lilac, Green, and the rest of the rainbow.

Almost as abounding in surprises was the periodicals section. I'd had no idea there were so many magazines. Hundreds of them, both popular and highly specialized, on wide racks, with long, polished wooden tables on which to examine them. There were always a good many adults at those tables. These were Depression years, and the library was clean, well lit, warm in the winter, and a place where, if you were out of work, you could at least improve your mind.

We were all strangers, but in the library, a common interest in an author or a subject got a kid and an adult to whispering. Even a black kid and a white adult. One of the regulars was a boy of about fifteen who looked like Stepin Fetchit and had read himself into being an expert on the American Revolution. Forever eager to talk about any aspect of the subject, he was also a ready source of recommended books and articles. Years later, I heard he had gone quite mad.

The library was such neutral ground that acolytes of Father Coughlin kept their epithets in their pockets when sitting across a reading table from a Jew with a yarmulke on. And to my continuing surprise I found it possible at the library, to talk with an Irish kid without being accused of having killed his Lord. Still, I made a point of leaving the place before he did, to avoid being ambushed with a sackful of books.

I knew only one other neutral ground when I was growing up a Boston boy. Under the purple-and-white flag of Boston Latin School, we were all united — the Irish, the Italians, the Jews, the Greeks, the Scots, the Armenians, the relatively few Yankees who still went there (the others no longer applied because all the rest of us were there), and the far fewer blacks.

Whatever part of the city we came from, each of us, because we were going to Boston Latin School, was a special kid on his own street. The other kids, going to ordinary high schools, might well growl that we were snooty beyond words, but they knew we had already gone a few laps around the success track while they hadn't finished one. So to be thrown out of Latin School would mean being put back into the common pool of common students — much to the delight of the common pool, and to the everlasting shame and humiliation of our parents, let alone us.

A lot of Latin School kids did get thrown back to the neighborhood high schools. As Theodore H. White, the chronicler of presidential campaigns and an alumnus of BLS, said in his memoir, *In Search of History:* "The Latin School was a cruel school. . . . It accepted students without discrimination, and it flunked them — Irish, Italian, Jewish, Protestant, black — with equal lack of discrimination."

Accordingly, the survivors, so long as they did survive, felt they had much, perilously, in common. It mattered more that we were long-distance runners under our purple-and-white colors than that we were Jews or Christians (in school, anyway). For the six years I was there, my closest friends were a Greek and an Irish lad. It took me a long time to believe that was possible.

The masters, moreover, paid no attention to where we came from, to whether our parents worked in grocery stores or were State Street bankers. The only thing that counted was whether we were willing to do the work, the incessant work, it took to stay in this place. If you stuck it out at

Latin School, where, after all, eight signers of the Declaration of Independence had gone, you knew there was really nothing you couldn't accomplish from then on — if you really put your mind to it.

This unrelentingly serious place is the oldest public school in America, in a three-story red-brick building with formidable Corinthian columns on the broad Avenue Louis Pasteur in the Fenway. There were masters so cold that a kind word from them seemed to be a terrifying trap. There was a sardonic, sharpshooting math teacher who kept a supply of small pieces of chalk on his desk from which he would select messengers to peg hard at a scholar's head to quicken his attention. I do not recall his ever having missed. Other masters were somewhat more amiable, but no master allowed for much familiarity. As Robert Wernick, an alumnus, wrote in the April 1985 *Smithsonian*, on the occasion of the school's three hundred fiftieth anniversary: "Even today when old graduates reminisce, you will rarely hear them say of any teacher, 'He really understood me.' They are more apt to say, 'He certainly taught me trigonometry and the ablative absolute.'"

After I left Boston Latin, I would occasionally complain about how uncaring most of the masters had been about our sensibilities, our souls. Finally, however, it occurred to me that they gave us something a good deal more important — respect. Whatever our backgrounds, we were in the school because we had shown we could do the work. The masters, therefore, expected at least that much of us, and that was why we came to expect even more from ourselves.

There were some fierce and suspicious Jews in my neighborhood who disapproved of Jewish boys discovering their potential in such a distant place. Distant not so much geographically, though Avenue Louis Pasteur was a far piece from Roxbury. But distant from Judaism. The whole point of this elite Latin School, these Jews said, was to produce one-hundred-and-fifty-percent-American boys. "So, if you send a Jewish boy there, he will forget what it is to be Jewish."

They might have been right if Boston Latin School had been all the world we knew. But on the trolley cars coming home, some of the parochial school boys growlingly reminded us we were Jewish, and back in Roxbury, at night, it was still foolish to go out in the dark alone. Back home, it still made a big difference where, in the old country, your parents were from.

My father hardly ever spoke about the old country. About himself as a boy in the old country. Since I thought we were both immortal, it never occurred to me there was a deadline for finding out about such things. He did mention that he had grown up where there was space, lots of space. Not in a shtetl but on a farm. His father's farm. It was hard, long work, but there was time, luminous time, for fishing and swimming. He was a strong swimmer. The only one of the ghetto fathers, when we went to the beach, who sometimes swam so far out that you couldn't see him anymore. The other fathers, as I do now, either slapped the water or floated — making very sure they were not over their heads. But my father, he didn't swim like a Jew at all.

"Once, there was a good bit of land in the family," a cousin of my father, one Chentov, who lives in London, told me some years after my father's death. "Your father's grandfather was a fierce old fellow who liked to ride around his land with a gun. It was strange enough that a Jew should be allowed to have land — but a Jew with a gun!"

Chentov had always meant to find out how all this happened, but, he told me, "I didn't ask until there was no one left to answer."

My father might have stayed where he was born, but the tsar wanted him in his army. So my father came to America, and in time was drafted by the President over here for the First World War. History was in need of my father.

He had come to America alone, at fifteen, traveling from Russia to Amsterdam, where he joined all the other strangers in steerage. On arriving in Boston, he made for the home of his eldest brother, a house painter and a spectacularly choleric man. The house painter gave the kid a cot to sleep on for a few days and then kicked him out. This, after all, was the land of independence. From then on, my father, having no other choice, made do with scraps of jobs. Eventually, he too became a house painter — a painter the contractors would pick first because he was so neat, conscientious, and quiet. Until he started butting into their business. Like how much they paid the painters, like whether anybody cared if a painter broke his neck on the job from a rotten rung on a ladder. My father organized a local of the house painters' union. God knows what the contractors would have done to him if the war hadn't saved him.

In France, my father was gassed. That experience, or something else, a doctor told him just before he was discharged, had left him with a heart condition. So he wouldn't feel too bad about that, the United States government awarded him a small disability pension.

Back home, which was Chelsea, a town near Boston, my father began to paint houses again. But he knew what his true vocation was and started saving to enter it. There are those obsessed with the law or jazz music or electronics. My father dreamed about haberdashery. As a young man, he was unfailingly dapper, and so he remained, though in a more subdued fashion, all the rest of his life. He was fascinated by what the right shade of blue in a shirt, the right cut of a jacket, the right snap of a hat, could do for a man. In business, and in love. And most important, in his own eyes. Like dentists who watch the destroyed teeth of passers-by on the street and fantasize the winning smiles that might have been under the right care, my father was certain he could improve anyone's life by advising him on how to dress.

After all, what were the two basic elements of success? Self-respect and the respect of others. And if you could add admiration to respect, success would be all the more abundant. A well-run haberdashery, therefore, would shape the present — and future — business, political, and even religious leaders of the community. He wanted that store.

And, in the mid-1920s, there it finally came to be, in Chelsea — Hentoff's Men's Shop. It soon acquired a quite distinctive reputation. "Cy knew what to stock," a traveling salesman told me. "You couldn't hype him. He bought only quality. And he knew the difference between quality that was not so expensive and quality that was overpriced. But the strange thing with Cy was how he would argue with the customers. Gently, you know the way he was, but stubborn. 'No, I won't sell this to you; you don't look good in it.' Or 'This is too expensive for what you really want.' I tell you, I used to stand there just to listen to this go on. On the road, the guys in the other stores, they wouldn't believe me. They wanted to know, 'What is he, a nut?'"

It worked, though. Of course it worked. Customers who had gone to another shop where they didn't need permission to buy what they wanted sometimes came home with fancy junk that stayed in the closet. So they became regulars at Hentoff's Men's Shop. And the word got around. Even goyim went out of their way to come. Including the mayor, an Irisher.

Those were my father's golden years, though he was still young. There was nothing about the store he didn't find absorbing. Arranging and rearranging the stock, taking inventory, keeping the books, inspecting the traveling salesmen's samples, feeling the weave. And in the middle of a weekday afternoon, when no one else was in the store, he'd just stand, his back to the door, looking slowly and lovingly at all the shelves and all the racks and all the display cases. How could the Russian boy, fishing in a lake on a farm, ever have imagined this!

My father had one other obsession: gambling. Poker. Pinochle. Twenty-one. Gin. And in the back room of Hentoff's Men's Shop, after hours, there was usually a game going on. You couldn't get badly hurt, all the players would say to anyone who asked, but you could get hurt. In fact, you could also get badly hurt. My father did.

Hentoff's Men's Shop might have survived the luck of the back room, but something else came along to sink the place. When the Great Depression began — only it was just "the Depression" then — it was hard for my father to believe that people would soon be so poor they'd make themselves do without any new clothes at all, not even accessories. But the store disappeared around 1933. When it collapsed he owed a lot of money. For stock he had bought on credit, for private loans he had taken in desperate stubbornness.

In the apartment in Roxbury, where I grew up, I used to see the separate ledger in which all those debts from the golden years were listed. He kept the ledger in a drawer, all by itself. For years he could do nothing but open the ledger once in a while and stare at it. But by the late 1930s my father was able to send some checks, and after the other war started, a good many more checks. By 1944 he had paid off all the debts, but he kept the ledger in the same drawer and still occasionally looked at it. I suppose he saw, in there, his magical haberdashery in the middle of a week-day afternoon.

My own entry into the work force came when I was eleven. Across the street from us there lived a fruit peddler. He had one son, who was my age, but whom we seldom saw in what meager time was left us Jewish boys every day for playing ball in the street. That one, the peddler's son, studied *all* the time. That one was going to attend the yeshiva and become a sage, like Rabbi Soloveitchik. That one was a peanut who couldn't have caught a ball anyway, even if you dropped it into his fayegele hand.

His father would not have dreamed for a second of taking his son away from his studies, but his father did need some help that summer. The father did not speak English, so one day, in Yiddish, he asked my father if I would be available. My father knew I was never reluctant to earn some money — I was already beginning to collect jazz records, although I didn't have a machine to play them on — so he said he would find out. My father was not of the school that believed children were fragile. The boy is in good health — why should he bum around during the summer? And in this job, he'd have plenty of fresh air besides. My mother had her own opinions but did not choose to share them. Anymore. A permanent minority in the house, she merely waited gloomily for the catastrophic results of every one of our decisions.

I accepted the position. The fun part was the horse. Riding high on the wagon, sometimes holding the reins, I was much envied that summer by all the boys on the sidewalks we regally passed by. Since the peddler could speak only Yiddish — a Yiddish so stuck together that I'd lose the thread in the first guttural rush — he and I did not speak at all.

So I talked to the horse. And waved at friends, and especially at enemies. What I was being paid for was to climb. Stairs. It was uncanny how often the women who bought the most fruit, particularly watermelons, lived on the top-most floors of their buildings. Sometimes they would tip, a nickel, and sometimes they would then put another nickel in the pushka — the blue-and-white metal box by the door — for trees in the coming Jewish homeland in Palestine. Maybe, as a Jew who already had a home, I was supposed to put my nickel in there too. So, there's one tree less in Palestine.

Nickels added up. I could make more than a dollar a day extra hauling the ladies' fruit upstairs. And the dollars added up. And sometimes, at the end of the week, I'd look at what I had and would remember something that had made a big impression on me a couple of years before. It was sort of an epiphany, you might say. This is the way it is, kid. This is the way the world works.

It was in the winter. My father, a traveling salesman by then, had just come back from an empty trip. Hats, felt hats, straw hats — who would buy such a thing in such times?

It was five-thirty, already dark, and I was sitting at the kitchen table, listening, as I did every day, to "Jack Armstrong, the All-American Boy" on the radio.

Wave the flag for Hudson High, boys,
Show them how we stand;
Ever shall our team be champions
Known throughout the land!

There was a knock on the door; my mother answered it, and a tall, thin, stoop-shouldered man in his forties announced matter-of-factly that he had come for the radio. Payments were four months behind and he was sorry, but he had his orders, and he reached his hand out to remove Jack, Billy, Betty, and Uncle Jim.

"Will you let the boy finish his program?" my father asked, without rancor, and without begging.

The man from the finance company nodded, sat down across from me at the kitchen table, accepted a glass of tea from my mother, and stared at me.

My father had rushed out the door, without a coat. He ran down Howland Street, up Elm Hill Avenue, which was a rather formidable hill, and arrived, breathing hard, at the apartment of one of my mother's sisters. The sister's husband, a dark, dour man, owned a string of dry-cleaning stores which were doing reasonably well despite the Depression. If you can't buy a new suit or dress, you treat what you have as an investment.

It was a loan of ten dollars my father was asking for. Not for him or for Lena. It was for Natie. The radio meant a lot to Natie. His brother-in-law rubbed his chin, looked at the ceiling, and said that it wouldn't be fair. "If I gave to you, Cy, I'd have to give to all the relatives in need, and Rockefeller I'm not."

Anyway, the man had left with the radio by the time my father came back, my request for one more quarter-hour for "Little Orphan Annie" having been rejected.

The silence in the apartment was scary. As if something awful had happened, which it had. Turning to my father, my mother finally broke the silence. "It's not your fault." He didn't say anything for the rest of the night. He didn't look at us, either.

My second venture into the work force took place when I was twelve. I didn't remember the name of the emporium until I saw it some years ago in my FBI files. (Anyone writing a memoir ought to take advantage of this free research service.)

The place was the W. Schwartz Haberdashery Store, and I got the job because Mr. Schwartz bought hats from my father. (Some people were buying new ones again.) Mr. Schwartz was round and hard, explosive in ordinary conversation and murderous when aroused. He had what used to be called a heavy Yiddish accent, which meant that if you knew no Yiddish, there was no way you could understand his English.

I was a stock boy, doubling as a salesman — to Mr. Schwartz's snorting apprehension — when the store was crowded. Boy though I was, I was not treated as a boy. I was one of the workers. I liked that. My father's role in my ascent to being a mensch was mentioned only on the first day, when W. Schwartz barked at me: "Cy says you're smart, so be smart and on time, and don't be a wise guy."

Near the end of that summer, I was fired. One morning, a customer, browsing around, picked out an expensive shirt. It was way overpriced, I thought, and I told him that it wouldn't wear nearly so long as some of our other, less expensive shirts. Just as I finished my helpful comments, a large, thick hand grabbed my shoulder as Mr. Schwartz whispered fiercely that I was immediately needed in the basement, *immediately,* and accelerated me in that direction with a vicious shove.

When the customer left, carrying the less expensive shirt I had recommended, W. Schwartz summoned me from the basement and then, without one more word, barreled over to the cash register, took out my week's pay, shoved the money at me, and walked right past me.

That night, my father and I argued. I insisted that I had done the customer a true service, not only saving him money but giving him greater — because more durable — satisfaction in what he had finally bought.

"That was not your decision to make," my father said.

"But you — you used to do just that when you had your store! Uncle Irving told me. You didn't want the customers spending any more than they had to."

"I could do that," my father looked at me. "It was *my* store. This is Schwartz's store."

D espite my failure to measure up to the standards of W. Schwartz, I went on the next year to audition for the premier boy's job in the neighborhood, a position at Sunday's Candies. Not just a summer job but work all year long — after school, weekends, and practically around the clock in the weeks preceding Christmas.

Sunday's Candies was to Fanny Farmer's, its nearest rival, as a Mercedes-Benz is to a Ford, as Muddy Waters is to the Rolling Stones, as Thomas Jefferson is to Jack Kennedy. From the chocolate on the outside to the myriad choice of fruits, nuts, and creams — just to begin with — on the inside, a Sunday's candy was a special event. Accordingly, all Sunday's purchases were specially wrapped, with ribbons specially tied. If the Queen of England had sent her footman in to buy a pound of the assorted, she would not have been disappointed in any detail.

The owner, in every way, of this chain of two candy stores was Samuel Caploe, a graduate of Harvard Business School and a pioneer of systems analysis long before the term had meaning outside our ghetto. By sheer manic intelligence and passionate devotion to detail, Mr. Caploe was more than qualified to be in charge of General Motors or General Foods or any of the giants of industry, singly or merged. But, through a cruel oversight of history, his managerial genius was focused on only two candy stores, with their dreamy women clerks during the day and, at all other hours, a bunch of boys who were essentially unappreciative wise guys.

Many more boys applied for jobs at Sunday's Candies than were hired. Applicants, to begin with, had to be at least fourteen, but some of us doctored copies of our birth certificates — so eager were we to be among the elect. A successful applicant had instant advanced status in the neighborhood. It was like being admitted to Harvard, where many of the Sunday's boys eventually did go. Getting behind Mr. Caploe's counter was getting on the fast track. As was well known in the lore of Roxbury and adjoining Dorchester, Mr. Caploe picked such smart boys that Sunday's Candies alumni were amply represented among the physicians, professors, lawyers, engineers, and judges of the Bay State. No one had ever heard of a Sunday's boy winding up a failure. A few were said to have married shiksas; but that was like catching a social disease — you couldn't blame Mr. Caploe for that.

Girls were preparing for and going to college even back then, but no female students were ever hired for Sunday's Candies. Women were seen behind the counter only during the day, and they were all employed from the general female work force. High school graduates, most of them married, their studies forever done with. Mr. Caploe never explained why he did not hire from the student body of Girls' Latin School or Radcliffe, but then no one ever asked him.

Every boy who applied for a job had two long interviews with Mr. Caploe himself. The first began with an examination of the applicant's soul. Not in any religious sense. Mr. Caploe wanted to know if this boy was honest, honest in every fiber of his being.

He started by immediately making eye contact with the applicant. Woe unto the child who looked down or up or anywhere but into Mr. Caploe's hotly shining eyes. "You let one shifty child into your operation," I once heard Mr. Caploe tell one of the women who worked days, "and you're a dead man."

The soul test, after a series of probes into our integrity since birth, always ended the same way. We knew because on slow nights we would compare notes with the newest clerks, and they affirmed that this part of the entrance exam never changed. Mr. Caploe would begin to set up the papers for the battery of intelligence tests that were coming up next, and the applicant, having screwed himself to the point of almost unbearable virtue, felt able now to relax.

"Oh, one more thing." Mr. Caploe's eyes were shining again. "I want you to think carefully. Take your time before you answer. Now, would you say it is wrong to steal a hundred dollars?"

Wrong? "Wrong" wasn't the word for so despicable a crime. Any boy who stole a hundred dollars should be publicly flogged in Franklin Park and made to spend the night with the snakes.

Mr. Caploe would nod. "Now, would you say that stealing an apple is as wrong as stealing a hundred dollars? Take your time."

Not one boy in the whole history of Sunday's Candies interviews had ever hesitated one moment to say indignantly that, of course, stealing an apple is as bad as stealing a hundred dollars. *Because* — and it was heartening to find out how many of us had used exactly the same words — *because* any boy who would steal an apple would *eventually* steal a hundred dollars.

Nodding with enthusiasm, Mr. Caploe then put us through two hours of assorted intelligence tests. (At the time, I should point out, Sunday's Candies clerks earned thirty-five cents an hour. And particularly outstanding clerks who were promoted to boy store managers — nights and weekends — earned forty-five cents an hour. Mr. Caploe was not about to squander such wages on just ordinary minds.)

Some years later, at college and in applications for other jobs, I had to take other batteries of intelligence tests, but after Mr. Caploe's they were a breeze. Since Mr. Caploe was not standardized, the tests weren't. Like everything else that had to do with Sunday's Candies, the tests were devised in the astonishing laboratory of Mr. Caploe's mind.

The second interview consisted mainly of digital dexterity tests. The customers deserved and expected swift service with not one piece of chocolate bruised in the handling. There was also the matter of the fiendishly intricate wrapping and tying procedures, which also had to be done in a snap. Some of the applicants did not survive this second interview because, being Jewish boys on the way to college, their fingers were skilled only in turning the pages of books. In panic, those fingers, during the dexterity tests, ran amok among the fudge balls. And the pitiful struggles of these boys to control a box of candy until it could be tied made one wonder if their mothers still tied their shoes for them. I, however, a skilled musician, who could handle the clarinet passages in "Marche Slave" while naming in my head every sideman who had ever played with Duke Ellington, had no difficulty with Mr. Caploe's finger-busting exercises.

There was only one more Caploe criterion to meet. Personal appearance. The clerks must be as sparkling as the candy, as the windows of the display cases, as the very sidewalk in front of the store. And I, to the ceaseless dismay of my father, constantly looked as if I were the apprentice to the herring man on Blue Hill Avenue. But to win *this* job, I appeared, for both interviews, well scrubbed, hair as carefully parted and smooth as Tyrone Power's, and dressed in a suit, white shirt, and tie. When I came home, my father, close to tears, said, "I'll never see you like this again."

The letter came. I was now on the fast track. Before being allowed to speak to a customer, however, I was put into training for a week, as had happened with new Sunday's Candies clerks from time immemorial. My instructor was a night store manager, a student of the history of religion at Harvard Divinity School by day and a student at all hours of the wholly uncategorizable Mr. Caploe.

During that orientation week, I learned how the candy was made — though not the secret formula — and was then guided through two huge books which all employees had to master. The first one, which had to be learned by heart, because Mr. Caploe gave the clerks and managers frequent spot quizzes on its contents, was called The Manual. It contained all the rules of the establishment. From the number of pieces of candy each clerk was allowed to eat per shift — one (1) — to a list of phrases that had to be used when talking to customers. No variations were permitted:

"Good morning (afternoon) (evening). May I help you?"

"Would you like this gift-wrapped?"

"Yes, the weather has been pleasant (unpleasant) (changeable)."

"I appreciate your point of view, Sir (Madam) (Miss), but I don't know anything about politics."

"Yes, the design on the top of each piece of chocolate tells what is inside it. Which would you like me to tell you about?"

The Manual also defined the relationship between store clerk and store manager. No fraternization during work hours, although both were boys. The clerk and manager were equal only in the number of sheets of toilet paper they were allowed per shift: ten (10) each.

The second thick volume consisted entirely of inspirational articles from various periodicals and books. Tales of self-made giants of industry who as boys, had parlayed pluckiness, utter truthfulness, and unquestioned loyalty to their employers — all of this having led to their present richly deserved and enjoyed eminence.

The two volumes were the only reading matter we were

permitted on the job. If all of our appointed tasks had been completed and if there were no customers in the store, we could take a bit of wholesome pleasure in testing our mastery of the rules in The Manual. Or we could dip into the second volume's exciting true adventures, which should make us proud to have this chance, at so early an age, to follow the path of these grandly self-reliant Americans. (Actually, as an admirer of Horatio Alger, I quite liked those stories, much to the scorn of some of my hipster colleagues.)

If, on the other hand, any of us were caught reading anything but these sacred books on the job, we would be drummed out of the service. Reading that did not directly bear on the improvement of a boy's work was reading that distracted the boy, who, being distracted, could be rude to a customer who could tell other customers about the rude boys behind the counter — and that is how Sunday's Candies would be brought to ruin.

We paid as much attention to this rule as we did to the equally insistent regulation that employees eat no more than one (1) piece of candy a night. We were all going to school, and whenever there was no business to take care of, we would take turns hiding in the back of the store with our textbooks or other assigned reading.

Reading illicitly, however, was a dangerous risk, for Mr. Caploe was enthusiastically given to making surprise visits to his stores, especially at night and on weekends, when the boys worked. "Visits" isn't quite the word, however. They were raids. He would park his car around the corner, hunch over, and start to run. The first we would know we were in for another lightning inspection was when one of us saw Mr. Caploe's high-crowned, pearl-gray felt hat skimming along the outside window of the store, like the fin of a shark, on its way to the door. All those years it never occurred to Mr. Caploe that he could have achieved total surprise if he'd only left his hat in the car. But then he might have caught cold.

With those few seconds warning, whichever boy was studying in the back — alerted by a desperate cough from the boy in front — had just enough time to toss his book into the garbage bag. There was, alas, a night when I was in the back of the store and Mr. Caploe, possessed by a hunch, actually put his hand into the garbage bag and, with a howl, immediately withdrew it, covered with blood. Earlier that evening I had tossed a broken water glass into that garbage bag. Failing to wrap broken glass carefully in heavy paper and put it into a separate container was a violation of The Manual, as Mr. Caploe reminded me at great length that night. He did not, however, plunge his hand into the garbage bag again, and my Greek grammar was never exposed, though from that moment on, it did have traces of our founder's blood on some of the pages.

Along with trying to trap covert readers, Mr. Caploe had an overflowing agenda on these raids. Like running his forefinger over the tops of the outside of the display cases in a passionate quest for dust. He also checked to see if any tray of candy was less than brimming; and if a customer came in, he scrunched himself into a corner — under the conviction that he had become invisible — and listened to every word we said to the customer. If we strayed, however slightly, from the lines allotted us in The Manual, we had to explain why in a seminar that Mr. Caploe conducted as soon as the customer left. No explanation was ever satisfactory.

As might be expected, the concentration required by these raids was so fierce that nothing could deflect or distract Mr. Caploe from his rounds. A few of my more daring colleagues, however, would occasionally test Mr. Caploe's power of concentration.

Staring at the chocolate-covered cherries, for instance, Mr. Caploe would automatically — he prided himself on being a gentleman — ask after our health before also asking why two of the candies were upside down.

"How are you, W.A.?" he would say. (Mr. Caploe always addressed us only by the first two letters of our last names. This neatly precluded even the possibility of any sort of personal relationship between him and any of the boys. When you call someone "W.A." all the time, it's hard to remember he's a boy at all.)

In any case, on some of those raids, W.A., after being asked the state of his health, would cheerily reply, "Fine, Mr. Caploe. They're sure it's cancer, but they think I might have another month or two."

"Glad to hear it." Mr. Caploe, staring at the display cases, had now found two more chocolate-covered cherries in unseemly positions. "W.A., I want you to come around here and see what you've allowed to happen with the chocolate-covered cherries. If you were a customer, and you saw the slovenliness of those candies right here — right *here!* — would you buy anything in this store, or would you speed yourself to the nearest Fanny Farmer's?"

"I would throw up, Mr. Caploe," W.A. spoke into the void.

"And right over here, look at the fudge balls. Bruised, bruised." Mr. Caploe kept talking in his customary nasal timbre. He also talked habitually out of the side of his mouth, like a mobster who had taken over a candy chain.

Invariably, on these delightful visits, Mr. Caploe would take particular care to see how well the clipboard duties had been carried out. Everybody on each shift had a long, narrow board to which a large clip was attached. From the very top all the way down to the bottom of the board were typed instructions, and these had to be followed in exact order, from the beginning to the end of the shift.

At the top of the clerk's board, for instance, were instructions on how to sweep the sidewalk, including how to hold the broom. Farther down, the clip instructed the clerk to wash his hands and then to wash the outside display cases, the inside display cases, his hands again, inside and out, and so into the evening.

On one very special occasion, all of us boys were invited to Mr. Caploe's home. We suspected that he had read in one of the journals of industrial psychology to which he was addicted that an employer could increase the efficiency of his work force if he showed his employees that he, just as they, had a home and family whose welfare, just like theirs, depended on the health of the business which nurtured them all.

As we were shown into the large Caploe kitchen, we were astonished — but why should we have been? — to see hanging on the wall next to the door a long, narrow board with a large clip attached to it. And sure enough, the board, line by line, described Mrs. Caploe's daily duties from the time she came into the kitchen each morning at seven-twelve. As we looked around the spacious kitchen, it was then no surprise at all that everything was in precise, shining order — pots, pans, cups, glasses, cutlery, and Mrs. Caploe herself.

There came a time, however, when this marvelously designed chocolate-covered industrial microcosm was blighted. By greed, as Mr. Caploe mournfully told the story through the years. The greed of those boys whom he was helping get through school. The greed, particularly and disgracefully, of one boy. The ringleader, who sowed greed in the other boys and then harvested it. H.E. was that boy.

Indeed I was that boy. We all knew how much money Sunday's Candies took in on each shift. Each store manager's responsibilities, at the end of his list of clipboard duties at closing time, included counting the cash and putting it into the safe. And the store manager would tell his clerks what the night's take had been, because, despite The Manual's command to the contrary, the store managers did fraternize with the clerks. Those could be long nights, so the older boys turned out to be the mentors of the younger ones about everything from calculus and the Wars of the Roses to why the Christian girls at Radcliffe had such milk-white skin. (Because, said one store manager, a Harvard divinity student, Christian families who send their daughters to a place like Radcliffe have money. Therefore, even during the Depression, their daughters had been nurtured from the start on ample amounts of milk and cream. Unlike some of the rather leathery Jewish girls from neighborhoods like ours.)

In any case, it was easy to add our knowledge of Caploe's night receipts to the financial data we extracted from the women who worked the day shifts. On top of all that were the bountiful profits Mr. Caploe enjoyed from various special days of the year. On Mother's Day and Thanksgiving Day, for instance, customers were lined up down the block, and five deep inside the store.

And Christmas — ah, Christmas! For several weeks beforehand, while we were still in school, we boys worked not only our regular evening and weekend shifts but also late into the night, every night, filling large orders from department store owners, factory owners, a number of banks throughout the Boston area, and other large-scale employers. A gift-wrapped one-pound box from the Tiffany's of candy stores appealed to these bosses as being far more tasteful to distribute to the workers than something as vulgar as a cash bonus.

There were so many orders to fill that as soon as we boys were on Christmas vacation from school, we worked not only evenings and late into the night but during much of the day as well.

Initially, we had no firsthand knowledge of Caploe's profits from this pre-Christmas assembly line manned by Jewish child-elves, because those receipts weren't part of regular store sales. But in our innocent desire to take even further pride in the resounding achievements of Mr. Caploe, we got the bookkeeper to brag, in detail, about the grand rush of income from the big special orders.

During my first year at Sunday's Candies, I started brooding about us boys being paid as boys while making very grown-up profits indeed for our employer. To the neighborhood, however, Mr. Caploe was our beloved benefactor. So many boys had worked their way through the very best schools because that man cared about those boys. On the other hand, I started saying to my colleagues behind the counter, how many of the adults praising Mr. Caploe's Boys' Town would themselves work for thirty-five cents an hour? (Forty-five cents if they were store managers.)

We boys needed a union. It did not seem likely that any of the unions I knew about would be interested in organizing a bunch of kids. So we would create our own union, and I, a store manager by then, organized it. Our demands would be simple. Ten cents an hour more for clerks, ten cents an hour more for store managers. And a bonus, the details to be negotiated, for our practically round-the-clock labors during the weeks before Christmas — an ordeal that must be in violation of state, federal, and God's child labor laws. In fairness, in decency, surely we should have a bonus. In cash, not in candy.

And if Mr. Caploe said no? We would strike. And that was the beauty part of our strategy. Our demands would be presented at the end of November. There would be a week for negotiations, but absolutely no extension. If he preferred to continue to abuse his child work force, we would walk out just as the big Christmas orders were coming in. There was no way Mr. Caploe could train enough scabs in time to fill those orders unless he didn't care that the candies would be squooshed into each other, fudge balls penetrated by chocolate-covered lemon peels, coconut balls drenched in pink sauce from smashed chocolate-covered cherries. But Mr. Caploe did care deeply about the quality of his product. He would have to surrender.

When I presented the demands, Mr. Caploe looked at me as if I had stolen both the apple and the hundred dollars. He was disappointed, terribly disappointed. In me, in the two boys with me, in all the boys who had entered into this cold, unfeeling conspiracy. It may be, it probably had been, a mistake for him to hire bright boys in the expectation that they were mature enough to understand the dynamics of business, the mutual trust between worker and employer that was at the heart of every successful enterprise.

We not only expected the speech, but for weeks we had taken turns delivering it, although no one had been able to get all the way through his impersonation of Mr. Caploe without breaking up. But on this day, in the real world of industrial relations, the three of us listened to Mr. Caploe's tale of sadly misplaced faith without expression. After a quarter of an hour or so, I said that we expected to hear from him before the deadline, but if we did not, we would do what we said we would do.

Mr. Caploe thought he had a way out. If he could turn the ringleader around, the rest of this kid union would collapse. Now, how do you get the ringleader to understand the injustice of what he is doing, the base ingratitude he is revealing? How do you get him to realize that he can destroy the company? If the business disintegrated, not only would those smart-alecky boys not get a raise, they would not have a job, and generations of worthy boys to come would not have a job at Sunday's Candies. How do you get common sense into that boy who calls himself a union organizer? You talk to his father.

Mr. Caploe called my father and asked if he could come to our home on a matter of great importance. He would rather not say what it was on the telephone.

That very evening, I looked out of my bedroom window and saw Mr. Caploe parking his car in front of the apartment house on Howland Street. And out he came — not on the run, as was his usual nocturnal custom; in fact, he just stood there for a while, tapping his high-crowned pearl-gray felt hat in thought.

In the living room, my father was drinking a tall glass of strong, scalding tea, a lump of sugar between his teeth. He offered a glass of the same to Mr. Caploe, but my employer, a more assimilated Jew, preferred coffee. Crouched in the hallway outside, I saw and heard it all.

Mr. Caploe, sounding as rabbinical as he could, spoke to my father of the painful, painful history of the Jewish people. "Yet, despite the agonies, the massacres, the expulsions, we have been able to do so much more than survive because — we *are* a people, we support each other, we do not abandon each other. In the important things, we trust each other. But H.E. — that is, Nathan — has forgotten what has kept us Jews together."

My father said it seemed to him that this was a labor dispute rather than a question of the survival of the Jewish people.

Mr. Caploe pushed the history of the Jewish people aside and spoke as one man with family responsibilities to another man with family responsibilities. If he were to yield to these boys, Mr. Caploe said to my father, then they would ask for more, and more. You could see it all over the place. Businesses closing down because of unions. What, after all, is to prevent these boys from blackmailing me every year at this time?

Trust, my father said. And a fair contract.

Mr. Caploe tried another route. Quite apart from the unfairness of this attack on him, quite apart from the selfishness of these boys, did my father think it was a good thing for his son to begin to get a reputation as a — how to put it? — a troublemaker?

"Actually," my father answered, "I think this shows a certain leadership quality in Nathan. That until now I wasn't sure he had. I also think that since these boys are doing a man's work and since you cannot get a man to do what these boys do for thirty-five cents an hour, Nathan is right."

Mr. Caploe, picking up his high-crowned gray felt hat, rose, thanked my father for the coffee, and started to leave.

"Tell me," my father said to him at the door, "where will you find replacements for the boys?"

Mr. Caploe glared at him. "Many boys will jump at the chance to work at Sunday's Candies."

"In this neighborhood?" my father said. "In this neighborhood, where is there a boy who will cross a picket line?"

There was no strike. We won our raise. We lost the demand for a cash Christmas bonus. Mr. Caploe said that would be giving away the store, and he would close down rather than submit. Next time, we said to ourselves, next time you'll submit.

But Mr. Caploe did continue his fabled Christmas present for each clerk and store manager — a one-pound box of candy. Each of us packed his own, mustering what strength we had left to jam the maximum amount of candy, and then some, into a one-pound box. Indeed, it was a chain-wide competition, open to all clerks and store managers, to determine the master candy-stuffer.

Traditionally, this tournament took place at each store when we were closing up on Christmas Day. The clerk or manager with the most candy, in whatever shape, in his

Christmas box won a prize: the esteem of his fellows, manifested in a rain of huzzahs, and three bonus gift boxes for girlfriends, mothers, or even aunts. The latter dividend was awarded in the name, if not by the express desire, of Samuel Caploe, who never did learn what we had made of his one-pound Christmas gift.

I had never won one of the Christmas prizes, but my last year at Sunday's I was sure I was going over the top. In a manner of speaking. By the rules, the one-pound box, no matter how many pounds actually wound up in it, had to be packed in a way that allowed it to be closed. My box weighed in at three and a half pounds. But I was topped again, this time by a new clerk whose grotesquely misshapen box contained four and a quarter pounds. The cover did not exactly fit two of the corners of his box, but it did stay on.

The store manager that evening, the longtime graduate student at Harvard Divinity School, awarded the prize. There were tears in our eyes — tears of exhaustion. The manager pointed to the new clerk and urged the rest of us, spent as we were, to recognize the spiritual significance of what had just happened.

"It is the faith demonstrated by this boy," said the store manager, "which should inspire each and every one of us. Granted there is a slight flaw in his completion of the task, but, my children, consider the power of the spirit that has been able to pack four and a quarter pounds of candy into a one-pound box. Let us pray that that spirit may enter into us. And may God bless us, every one!"

On Washington Street, one of Boston's least gracious but liveliest thoroughfares, there was a place of music, Krey's. Instruments, sheet music (a very big item back then, when folks still actually played the piano at home), and recordings. Over the door was a speaker from which, all day long, at jarring volume, came the newest releases of the big dance bands whose leaders and singers were the pop stars of the 1930s — a time when a father and his kids sometimes liked the same sounds.

In my tenth year, walking by one summer morning, with hours to go before my shift at Sunday's Candies, I was suddenly stopped by a fierce wailing of brass and reeds, a surging, pulsing cry of yearning that made me cry out too. I'd never before yelled in public; it was not something a Boston boy, especially a Boston Jewish boy wandering outside the ghetto, could ever satisfactorily explain to one of *them*. But I didn't care. All I cared about were those sounds.

I rushed into Krey's to find out what was playing. Artie Shaw's "Nightmare." The guy behind the counter at Krey's, Bill Ingalls, had a jazz radio show. He told me when it was on, and from "Nightmare" I went on to much more astonishing pleasures — Duke Ellington's "The Sergeant Was Shy," Louis Armstrong's "West End Blues," Billie Holiday's "Miss Brown to You." Not only could I hear in this jazz the soul-shaking power of the chazzan and the spiraling risks of his improvising, but here there were also such inviting sensuousness, the sharing of hip wit, and the colors — my God, there were more different colors in this music than in all of the Boston Museum of Fine Arts.

And the way the music moved! I'd be walking down the street and suddenly Fats Waller would leap into my head, from a record I'd heard that morning, and I'd be walking differently down that street. Or George Brunies would take over:

> I may be late
> But I'll be up to date
> When I can shimmy like my sister Kate —
> I'm shoutin' —
> Shimmy like my sister Kate!
> Oh, boy.

And I'd be strutting down that street.

When I got a record player, on time, I discovered that in and around Scollay Square there were secondhand bookstores that also sold cut-out records. My jazz universe kept expanding: Bessie Smith, Peetie Wheatstraw ("The Devil's Son-in-Law"), Jack Teagarden, Sidney Bechet. But it wasn't enough. I had to *see* the music; I had to see the musicians.

Acting as if I had no reason to ask what the minimum age was, and already needing a shave practically every day, I went to Sunday jam sessions in downtown Boston at the Ken Club. A dark, sleazy joint, but on those afternoons it was utterly transformed into a glorious battlefield, a tournament of giants, horn-playing giants. Like Wild Bill Davison, whose trumpet always sounded as if it were on the verge of disorderly conduct. He had the look of someone who'd hung out with every major gangster of the 1920s and had outdrunk them all. The vibrant force with which Wild Bill played made it impossible for any other horn to stand up to him in blazing ensemble passages.

Until Sidney Bechet came to one of those Sunday bashes at the Ken Club. Chunky, his moonlike face furrowed and stubborn, Bechet raised his long, straight soprano to his lips and there came forth a shout, a mighty passion, an *insistence* on dominating the universe, that clashed head-on with Wild Bill's ferocious zest for dominion. Neither did yield that afternoon—thoroughly exhausting the listeners, who were, however, still not satiated.

It was not until I was fifteen or so that I found the courage to actually speak to jazzmen, and some of them —unknown to my father—eventually became my itinerant foster fathers. Rex Stewart, Ben Webster, Frankie Newton. I admired them and carefully considered their advice on how to grow up, because they had so much life in them by contrast with practically all the other adults I knew. And whenever I heard their music, I still wanted to shout aloud—for the surprise and joy of it. The only other person who made me feel like that was a fiercely devout Catholic muckraking journalist, Frances Sweeney.

She understood what jazz gave me that Boston Latin School didn't, and the kids I knew didn't, and for sure my family didn't. My mother, bewildered as my stacks of recordings expanded into the living room and along the walls in the front-hall corridor, could only say: "Why do you keep buying more? They all sound the same."

And at the Ken Club, on those Sunday afternoons, I

would see women my mother's age, but they were American. American born. And they were gracefully dressed. And they showed, in the way they looked and listened, how subtly and accurately they understood this music that went way beyond music. There was no way I could imagine my mother sitting there. But then I hardly knew my mother, as I was to find out long after.

At home there was a photograph, a sepia print, of my mother. It was taken around 1920, soon after she had been promoted to cashier at Filene's, a large, bustling Boston department store known for the crisp alertness of its employees. And so my mother looked in the photograph: a crisply efficient, slender, dark-haired stranger in her early twenties.

Three years later she had married. "She had always wanted a blond," one of her younger sisters remembered sixty years later. "She fell in love with one when she worked in another department store, before Filene's. A Swede. She was crazy about him. But, of course, it couldn't happen. I told her, 'Lena, you can't do it. Father would die. He would drop dead.' And Lena said, 'I'm not going to do it.' She left the Swede, and she left the store. Lena would never do anything to hurt her family."

In time, Lena Katzenberg found and married a Jewish blond. A tall Jew with wavy blond hair and green eyes who had also come from Russia. A gregarious but serious man who, according to members of her family, was a nice guy but not nearly so smart as Lena.

The brightest student in her high school senior class, she had — one of her sisters told me with undiminished pride long after Lena was dead — recited Tolstoy at her graduation. When the principal found out Lena was not going to go on with her studies, he went to see her father, a tailor, and pleaded with him to convince his daughter to nurture her special qualities. The tailor, who worked very long hours but was never able to stay ahead of the month's rent, told the caring principal that his daughter could not go on with her studies. "I know her qualities," my grandfather said, "and that is why I know she will help to support this family."

It was after she died — my mother and I almost never spoke about her past — that I was told what happened after her father died. There were no sons. Of the daughters, one was older than my mother, and two younger. Not one of the four knew enough Hebrew to recite Kaddish — the mourner's prayer — so that it would be more than syllables strung together by rote. And the widow, though as strong and stubborn as a yoke of oxen, knew less Hebrew than her daughters.

In any case, among Orthodox Jews, women were — and are — not permitted to say Kaddish. If no men in the family are left to mourn — no son, no brother-in-law, no uncle — then the women arrange to have a Kaddish zager (a Kaddish sayer) function as the surrogate official mourner. He can be found in a synagogue or at a Yeshiva.

My mother would have none of that. Well, almost none.

My mother, around 1926. Courtesy of Janet Krauss

My parents, Lena and Simon Hentoff, in 1952.
Courtesy of Janet Krauss

She needed a Kaddish zager until the tutor she hired had taught her enough Hebrew so that she herself could say the prayer — three times a day until the end of the eleventh month (plus one day) after the death. Thereafter, once a year, as the law commands, she said Kaddish at the yahrzeit, the anniversary, of her father's death. One of my oldest memories is of the yahrzeit candle at home, burning for twenty-four hours in a squat glass. All through my childhood I was afraid of those candles. It was like having Death himself in the house, lurking behind the flame.

For this young woman to have insisted on saying Kaddish for her father was more than remarkable back then. It was nearly revolutionary in our Orthodox ghetto, and obviously it took an extraordinarily self-confident, brave spirit to not so much defy as ignore centuries of male exclusivity in the ritual of death.

I know of this self-confident woman only through report and rumor. By the time she had become my mother, she seemed subdued, withdrawn. There was no link that I could see between the brisk young woman in the sepia print, whom I imagined striding purposefully through downtown Boston, and my mother. It was my worried mother whom I actually saw coming home from one of her occasional shopping trips downtown and telling of the baleful goyim she had seen, across the subway tracks, whispering about her as she moved out of their sight.

Boston being so fertile a breeding ground for anti-Semites, my mother might well have been a most accurate observer on those trips. But the young Lena I'd heard about would have stared down the creepy goyim and maybe joined the Anti-Defamation League to do battle with them wholesale, or bought a book on the psychology of rabble. My mother, however, brooded and made dinner.

I do not know what changed her from the young woman in the picture. "A very strong person, your mother," an old woman who had worked with her at Filene's once told me. "And such a cheerful girl. She had so many beaus, and she loved to dance. Loved to."

At bar mitzvahs, at weddings, I never saw her dance.

Once, though, I did see my mother act with bold self-confidence, and I hated her for it.

On Howland Street, in the apartment house across the courtyard from ours, lived a partner in a haberdashery. He was on the first floor, like us. Every Wednesday night, he and his wife presided over a high-spirited low-stakes poker game. My father, when not on the road, was a regular in the game. (He was a regular in a lot of games. One of my aunts used to say, "Everybody likes Cy, he's such a nice guy. He plays cards just about every night. He is a sick man about cards.")

I was ten, lying in bed on one of those Wednesday nights, listening to the laughing and kidding, hearing my father's cigarette-cough across the courtyard. In our apartment, the lights were off on those Wednesday occasions. My mother would sit at the kitchen table, muttering, looking directly into the kitchen across the way where the game was being held. This night, her muttering grew more and more rapid, then stopped entirely. The apartment became so quiet that I went into the kitchen to see if my mother was all right. I was just in time to see, through the window, my mother rush into the kitchen across the courtyard and, without a word, overturn the table — cards, chips, sandwiches, glasses, spilling onto the floor. Still silent, she left. I ran back to my bedroom, feeling so humiliated for my father, wanting to say something to him, knowing that would have made it worse. She, she who had caused him this shame, was back in the black kitchen, muttering.

In all the time I lived in that apartment, my father never invited any of his friends home. Not even one of his various bosses. Relatives came from time to time, but so did the iceman, and the shammash from the shul for the payment on my long-since bar mitzvah. And that was my mother's social life: the relatives, the iceman, the shammash. When my father was on the road, which was often, she never went out at all in the evening. When he was home, he would sometimes take us both to the movies, but many nights Cy, whom everybody liked, was sitting with friends at somebody's table waiting for the card that would make gin. He also saw many daylight friends in the course of his travels —his customers in their stores from Pawtucket to Bangor; other traveling salesmen en route; night clerks at hotels. Although it could be exhausting, my father was fond of moving from town to town. And he was fonder still of telling about his travels while he played cards at other people's houses, a glass of cream soda and a corned beef sandwich at his side. It was a pretty good life.

I am surprised, now, that during those years, all my mother did was overturn just one card table. One lousy card table. My father was a lucky man. Much, much luckier than the young woman in the sepia print.

In all of Boston, the woman I most admired, sometimes feared, and ridiculously loved was Frances Sweeney. In her early thirties, the only daughter of a saloon keeper, she had long pale blond hair and deep blue eyes that could be unbearably cold or joyfully defiant, as when she was thrown out of a neo-fascist meeting in 1941 for heckling the speakers. She was also, however, perfectly at ease at high tea with a Boston Brahmin.

I went to work for her when I was fifteen. Frances Sweeney was the owner and editor of a newspaper, the *Boston City Reporter*, whose only purpose, at its start, was to put corrupt politicians in prison. In the Boston of the late 1930s and early 1940s, that looked to be as easy as shooting fish in a barrel.

There was a problem, however, in getting the paper out on a regular basis. While newsstand sales were desperately high at City Hall and at the State House, there was not all that much interest in the *Boston City Reporter* elsewhere in Boston. The citizens saw local politics as an extension of the comic pages, and therefore hardly worth serious indignation. Accordingly, the paper, its cash flow down to a trickle, was sometimes late in appearing, Fran Sweeney having had more than the usual difficulty in swinging a loan.

She refused to take ads, not that any responsible commercial institution would have risked setting itself up as a target for politicians skewered in her news pages. But Fran did not even want to consider the possibility of temptation if, at a time when money was nowhere to be found, an advertiser offered to take another page to help bail her out. She refused to be beholden to any outside party, even if the party asked nothing of her but a chance to buy space. "After all," she said, "what if that advertiser turns out to be crooked? *Then* who gets tarred? You're damn right. Me!" Furthermore, with no advertisers, and none of their money to learn to depend on, none of the thieves she wrote about could ever try to pressure the *Boston City Reporter* through its advertisers.

No one in the world could have successfully pressured Fran. "No one," she liked to say looking in the mirror, "can go past me to my boss." Gravely, she would bow to herself in the mirror. "*I* am my boss."

Her sole paid employee was a tall, cadaverous Greek named Gus. (I learned elsewhere that his full name was Constantine Aristides Gazulis.) He had a black military mustache, wore a slouch hat pulled down over his black hair and eyes, and seldom revealed anything about himself.

Coming from Roxbury, where the full range of left sectarianism thrived, with attendant highly specialized historians, I was able to find out that Gus was an obsessive record keeper of individuals and groups specializing in racial and religious bigotry. He had also been active in labor politics until pushed out by the Stalinists. "If you're ever going to be of any use to the labor movement," Gus once told me in his customary whisper, "never leave a union meeting early. Be the last one to go—then even if you can't stop what the Stalinists do, you'll know how they did it."

Gus was Fran Sweeney's main investigator for the political corruption stories. She had other sources deep inside the city and state bureaucracy — "the ones who aren't getting their share," she'd explain — but she also needed Gus to check *their* information, although she did a lot of that too.

He was a soundless man. I mean, he moved through the streets and alleys and courtyards of Boston like a ghost, a ghost who loved to surprise his friends. Gus, for instance, had the most disconcerting trick of suddenly appearing right behind your ear — in the reading room of the main branch of the public library, on a jammed street corner on Washington Street, or on a deserted stretch of the Fenway in the Back Bay. He had not been in sight a half-second before, and often you had not seen him for days, but there he was, behind your ear, whispering, "What's doing, kid?" It was a one-way question, of course, because if you asked *him* what's doing, he would, like the Cheshire Cat, fade away.

As quietly useful as Gus was, Fran Sweeney needed to add to her staff when she decided to expand the *Boston City Reporter*'s coverage to include anti-Semitism. As a serious Catholic, well ahead of the Second Vatican Council in this matter of not blaming the Jews for the Crucifixion (among a good many other things), Fran saw anti-Semitism as an abomination, a direct scandal to the faithful which the faithful had to combat. Above all people, Catholics, especially in Boston, had reason to know what an affront to God it was to stigmatize anybody because of his religion or race or whatever. And the pain of it. The humiliation of it. No dogs or Irish allowed! "Don't you *remember*?" she would ask those of her faith, including the priests.

That's what infuriated Sweeney. That Boston was the most anti-Semitic city in the country. And why? Because of Catholics! Because of the thousands and thousands of Catholic households where Father Coughlin's *Social Justice* was distributed and savored every Sunday. And sold in front of Catholic churches! And where was the denunciation of this priest of hatred? Not from the pulpits of the Catholic churches. Not in the parochial schools. Not in the *Boston Pilot.* And though the leader of the flock, the arctic William Cardinal O'Connell, disdained Father Coughlin, he stopped short of condemning his teachings.

As Anthony Lukas has noted in *Common Ground,* "Just as Pope Pius XII failed to condemn Hitler's concentration camps, so when bands of Irish youths ranged Blue Hill Avenue (they called it 'Jew Hill Avenue'), harassing and beating Jews, the Cardinal was conspicuously silent."

It was necessary, therefore, to confront the entire city, especially its Catholics, with the foulness of the anti-Semitism that was flourishing in Boston. Sweeney needed to reveal the sources, ideological and financial, of this epidemic, so that all souls would be shocked out of their complacency or complicity.

She needed more reporters. She could pay nothing, so she asked a couple of young Jewish socialists whom Gus knew to recruit other young Jews. Who would be more fiercely motivated to dig up this news than the victims?

I was one of the recruits, suggested by one of Gus's socialists in my class at Boston Latin School. There were about a dozen of us volunteer scourges of the anti-Semites, and before we were given our assignments, Frances Sweeney, sitting on a table in front of us, said:

"What I want from you is facts. A fact is something that can be proved, and you will bring me the proof with each fact you bring me. Anything that is not a fact is an opinion. I do not want your opinions. In this newspaper, only the editor has opinions, but they are of no use unless they are based on facts. You understand, then, how important you are, and how much damage you can do if you're careless, if your facts turn out to be lies. That's all our enemies will need to discredit the whole lot of us. You understand?"

I did, I did. I listened to the first editor I'd ever had with unreserved respect as I wondered what it would be like to put my arms around this small-waisted savior of my people.

One of my assignments was undercover. I had to report on an anti-Semitic tribe of Israel. Actually, it was a tribe of Israel that claimed to have gotten lost way back then. Indeed, it was the only *legitimate* tribe of Israel. Its members, the true Chosen People, were coming together now to prepare for the day when they would officially proclaim, far and wide, that the Jews were slimy impostors, not Israelites at all but jackals who had never had a land of their own and concocted *their* version of the Old Testament to pretend that they had. This *authentic* tribe, having gloriously found itself, would soon claim its rightful real estate in Palestine.

Fran wanted to know more about these true Israelites because Gus had leads indicating the long-lost tribe was financing some of the nuttier anti-Semitic pamphleteers in the city. The true Israelites figured that as Jews came to be increasingly hated, there would be rising support from true Americans for the land claims of the lost tribe.

Most of the tribe's meetings were closed, but a few were

opened to test the waters of response out there. However, the visitors allowed into the open meetings were carefully screened to sort out Jews pretending to be Israelites, and others hostile to history. But a fifteen-year-old Greek did not stir any suspicions. Shielding a small pad and a much smaller pencil, I wrote down the names of the speakers, what they said, described them, and casually collected all the literature I could find. I also noted that most of the members of the lost tribe seemed to be German or Scandinavian. Most of them, moreover, appeared plumply prosperous.

When I got back to the paper, Gus snatched the names and descriptions with what, for him, was glee, and later they became a small part of a story in the *Boston City Reporter* on the local funding sources of the hate sheets.

After a while I lost track of the tribe, but in the mid-1980s there was much news about a heavily armed network of anti-Semites in the West that called itself, as an ensemble, the "Identity Movement." Some also use the common identification "The Aryan Nations." Among them are souls on fire who claim they are descended from a lost tribe of true Israelites, but the territory they want now — as widely reported in the press — is the whole of America, which must be purged of Jews:

"We are the people of the race of G-d; the Talmudic Jew is the chosen people of the Satan. We are the front line of life and liberty; the Jew is the cauldron of death and enslavement. We do not want any other race to be present in our land at any time."

I don't know whether any of the latter-day true believers are the children of the rather genteel anti-Semites whose meetings I infiltrated for Fran Sweeney. I am quite sure, however, that the penalty now for being unmasked as a fake Israelite among them would be memorable.

In addition to writing about the Jew haters around the city, Fran Sweeney also focused on the indifference of the Church to the involvement of Catholics in this reviling of the Jews. In the *Boston City Reporter,* Fran Sweeney asked Cardinal O'Connell, again and again, when he would tell the faithful, without equivocation, to stop persecuting the Jews.

At last the Cardinal was heard from. He summoned Fran Sweeney to his presence. I had never seen her afraid before, but when she left that morning, she was pale and stiff with foreboding. The bearer of the message from the Cardinal had told her, out of the side of his mouth, that the Cardinal said he had finally lost patience with this enemy within the Church. And when this Cardinal lost his patience, the earth moved.

He had been Cardinal since 1911. His parents had worked on the looms of the Lowell mills, but you would never know that to hear his frostily upper-class speech. A musician and composer, the Cardinal was a connoisseur of other arts as well, and like nearly every man of God in Boston and its environs, he had his politics. Conservative politics. He had even voted Republican from time to time.

O'Connell could be charming to other aristocrats, but most people found him distant; and when he was angry, the Cardinal turned to ice. He had no liking for Father Coughlin because, for one thing, one of his firmest convictions was "The priest has his place and he had better stay there." And being on the radio all over the country, talking about politics and the Gold Standard, is not the place of a priest. Nor was the Cardinal receptive to anti-Semitism. It was all so vulgar. He had had enough, however, of this woman hectoring him about the so-called weakness of his response to Coughlin and his response to this thing among the faithful about the Jews.

When Fran came back a few hours later, she was still pale, but her jaw was set and her eyes were fierce. She would not tell us what had happened, but Gus did the next day. Fran had refused to bend. She would not promise to stop what the Cardinal called her recklessly irresponsible attacks on the Church. She had gone beyond all permissible, indeed rational, grounds, the Cardinal had told her. The facts are the facts, she replied. Silence is a fact, she added, especially when it comes from on high. Freezingly, from a great distance, William Cardinal O'Connell informed this woman that if her defiance continued, she could be in peril of excommunication.

"He wouldn't!" said a young Catholic woman, an assistant to Fran.

"He can," said Gus, "and when he speaks, he means to be obeyed. Still, it could be that Fran shook *him* up some. I don't know that he wants her entirely outside his command."

Fran heard nothing more from the Cardinal, and in her paper she kept reminding the priests of Boston and their Cardinal of their duty as Christians.

The Cardinal and the priests were eventually relieved of the scrutiny of this most unwelcome lady. Fran had had a rheumatic heart since childhood. Her doctor kept telling her that running the *Boston City Reporter* would be the end of her, and she would not bend to him, either.

One rainy night in April 1944, after she had put the paper to bed, Fran was walking home, alone, along Beacon Street, then as now one of Boston's most respectable thoroughfares. She had an attack and fell, still conscious, into the gutter. She could not move or speak, but she could hear. For a long time Frances Sweeney, the rain falling on her, listened as diverse Bostonians walked by, some ignoring her entirely, others shaking their heads and muttering about drunks being underfoot just everywhere these days. A cop finally took a second look at her.

She came back for a while but the slender troublemaker with deep blue eyes died in June of that year. She was thirty-six. (Gus died four years later, also thirty-six. He too had a rheumatic heart.)

When I heard of Fran's death I went home and played, not blues, but ballads by Ben Webster, the most gently passionate spirit in all of jazz. To my mother's mounting concern, I played the same records over and over for hours. I did not tell her why I was playing them.

A week later, as I was walking down Washington Street, a whisper, without warning, sounded in my ear.

"What's doing, kid?"

Gus didn't wait for an answer. "Come on, I'll take you to Felicani."

Aldino Felicani, a printer, had founded the Defense Committee for Nicola Sacco and Bartolomeo Vanzetti. He was a revered presence on the non-Stalinist left, and Gus had been promising to take me to his shop so I could tell my children I had met Felicani.

It was a large, dark room with a very high ceiling that diffused the gloom; and with well-used machinery all over the place, the feeling was that of a scene in Dickens where a boy begins his apprenticeship in surroundings that are intimidating but not entirely unfriendly.

Near a window sat Felicani. He seemed very old to me, but anybody over fifty did then. All I remember of his face were his eyes, which were smiling and skeptical. The combination was unnerving.

"What is he?" Felicani hooked his thumb in my direction.

"Socialist," Gus coughed.

"What else is he?"

"He's going to school; he works in a candy store."

"And after?"

"He wants to be a writer."

"No trade?"

"No trade."

Felicani shook his head and turned to me. "You know, this thing of being for others, of taking apart the whole damn system, is for a lifetime. Or it's no good. People who work only in here" — he tapped his forehead — "they forget."

"I won't forget, Mr. Felicani," I said, feeling foolish as I said it.

The printer smiled. "You won't be able to prove it by me." And he patted me on the cheek.

By the time I was granted my fleeting audience with Felicani, I considered myself, at sixteen, as knowledgeable about politics as I was about the Boston Red Sox and the Duke Ellington band. In my neighborhood, from the herring man standing beside his barrel and the excited yeshiva students sipping scalding tea through lumps of sugar at Segal's Cafeteria to my father and his friends, politics was the schnapps of daily conversation.

In national politics, most of us regarded Franklin Delano Roosevelt as an honorary Jew. In our ward, he took ninety-six percent or more of the vote every time. In my home, standing on the radio was a brass clock in the center of a ship's wheel, and steering that wheel was a grandly determined FDR. He was standing, of course. (We did not think of him as crippled.) At the base of the clock were the words "Roosevelt at the Wheel of the New Deal." My father had won that clock, early in Roosevelt's first term, at an amusement park outside Boston. It had long since stopped running, but it would never have occurred to my father, my mother, or me to throw it away. The country might have stopped running.

There were no Republicans in my neighborhood. None that I ever met. A few votes were cast for Republican candidates, but I figured those were by Jews with mental disturbances or Communists who wanted to hasten the Revolution by making Republicans as visible as possible.

In the spectrum of the ceaseless political debate in our ghetto, the FDR Democrats were the moderates — some would have said the conservatives. There were also much smaller but fiercely voluble bands of Communists, Trotskyites, and anarchists (the nonviolent kind who believed their pamphlets would be incendiary enough). We had single-taxers too, and more different flavors of socialists than ice cream.

All of them being true believers, they were constantly fishing for souls. A barbershop near where I lived was owned by a young, hard-working, cheerful, newly married soul who preferred talking baseball to politics but occasionally let it be known that FDR, for all his charm, was just another capitalist, and you'll see, all we'll get from him is the crumbs from his table.

The second chair was held by a gentle, soft-spoken man in his early sixties. He was the one who cut my hair. We would solemnly speak of such verities as the compelling social need for all landlords to be put in jail, all workers to join a union, and other such Roxbury small talk. One morning, when I was about thirteen, I heard from behind my head, "Nathan, you ought to start thinking about joining the Young Communist League."

Being full of horror stories about Stalin from local Trotskyites, I demurred, telling my friend the barber that I just wasn't cut out for party discipline. He kept after me. In the years ahead, he said, so much had to be, and would be, changed in this country. There could be no room for neutrals. Each and every one of us would be either part of the liberation of the masses or the enemy of the masses. It would be such a shame to see a nice boy like you, Nathan, on the list of the enemies.

I asked him if the enemies of the masses would be shot here too. My barber didn't like the question. And when the session was over, I didn't like the haircut. I kept going to the shop for the next six months or so, doing research into Lenin and Stalin before each visit. Eventually, the arguments and the way my head looked became so unpleasant that I found another barbershop. I never told my parents about the attempt to convert me. It didn't seem remarkable enough to discuss.

Politics, in any case, was of less compelling interest to me in those immediate post–bar mitzvah years than jazz, the Boston Red Sox, and the girls, mostly dark but a few golden, of our ghetto. That is, until Arthur Koestler's *Darkness at Noon.* I read it the summer I was seventeen. That one book, about all the Stalins in all the centuries, immunized me from then on against any variant, anywhere in the world, of the credo that infects both executioners and victims in *Darkness at Noon:* "The only moral criterion we recognize is that of social utility."

Many years later, at the Cuban Mission to the United Nations, I was asking Che Guevara when opposition parties might be allowed in Cuba. He smiled, as one might at a question from a retarded child. He didn't answer. He just smiled.

We did have a few polite disagreements on other matters, such as the counterrevolutionary notion that there ought to be an opposition press, even in a country next door to a hostile colossus. Finally, I said that had I been a Cuban, I would surely have supported Fidel when he was in the mountains but that within the first year of his victory I'd have been jailed. Guevara laughed before his interpreter had begun to translate my prediction. Handing me a cigar,

Guevara confirmed the likelihood of my fate but added that in Cuba there was plenty of room for argument among those who wanted the revolution to survive. There had to be such argument, he said, for ideas to be tested.

In *The Writer and Human Rights,* Thomas Hammarberg, secretary-general of Amnesty International, tells of a poem smuggled out on cigarette paper from Libertad Prison in Uruguay:

> You should see
> the contradictions
> in the army.
> You should have heard
> the arguments between
> the sublieutenants and the captain
> while they were torturing me.

Back then, in Roxbury, I would ask the neighborhood Stalinists, including some in knickers, about what Koestler had said about the terror in the USSR. Koestler was a well-known Fascist, I was told, and all those who had disappeared in the land of the future were also well-known Fascists. After a while they tired of this game. They gave up on me politically. My alleged passion for black music notwithstanding, I was an unredeemable bourgeois individualist. It was even bruited about, accurately, that I read P. G. Wodehouse.

As for me, I decided that when you know exactly what someone is going to say in answer to every single question you ask, you ought to put your nickel in some other machine. But these childhood friends and I talked about those things that still linked us — the lashing power of Ted

Williams, the girl on Elm Hill Avenue who kissed like a shiksa (from what we knew of shiksas in our dreams); and what Mrs. Nussbaum had said on the Fred Allen show last Sunday night.

By 1948, I was living outside the ghetto but came back every week to see my parents. It became known around Grove Hall that I was bad-mouthing Henry Wallace, the people's candidate for president. That I was saying the Commies in his campaign were playing him like a yo-yo. I owned up to saying that, and more. And that did it. For months — in one case, years — boyhood pals crossed the street when I came along. Others simply sneered. The one thing worse than a scab was a Red-baiter.

In 1983, William Phillips, the editor of *Partisan Review* and a tenured intellectual of the New York school, wrote a memoir: *A Partisan View: Five Decades of the Literary Life.* In it he mentions a meeting he arranged in the late 1960s between Norman Podhoretz and me, among others. It was one of Phillips's attempts "to reconstruct the intellectual community." It failed, for neither Podhoretz nor I would include the other in any intellectual community either of us wanted to be in. But in his memoir Phillips adds Podhoretz's characterization of me as a political innocent, particularly in my "lack of concern with the evils of Stalinism."

William Phillips lets that characterization stand, as if it were accurate. My elderly barber, had he lived so long, would have chuckled. "You see, Nathan, your betrayal of the masses did you no good."

I try, from time to time, to explain to my children how joyful politics used to be. The parades, the bands, the balloons, the buttons, the signs and stickers all over the place, and, above all, the candidates right in front of you. Not in a box in your home but in the neighborhood meeting hall or on a street corner or in a bar. You could see, right in front of you, who was brave and true. And you could see, you could actually see, those seekers of office from whose lips lies flew so naturally that they came even when not at all needed.

My father traveled so much that he hardly ever had the time to take me to Red Sox games, but he somehow did manage, most of the time, to be off the road when the political season began — the Democratic primaries. In Boston, the political season began and ended with the Democratic primaries.

During the campaigning, my father would take me to the candidates' nights at the Aperion Plaza, the neighborhood one-stop for social activities: bar mitzvahs and weddings, the High Holidays, banquets, and political appearances.

The Stalinists, the Trotskyites, and other swimmers against the mainstream never came to the candidates' nights, for they did not regard these tournaments as serious politics. They were low entertainment for the politically uneducated masses.

For me, those evenings at the Aperion Plaza were indeed entertainment, more flavorsome than most vaudeville. Also, for me and everybody else in the hall — from the exuberantly cranky neighborhood doctor to the herring man — having the candidates court us meant that we had a say in the affairs of the city and the state. We must matter to somebody besides ourselves, or they wouldn't have come.

The nights were long because there were many candidates for a considerable range of offices, but my father, even when there was school the next day, let me stay and listen to all of them. Then, on the way home, my father and I would grade them — first for content, but also for style, especially wit. And we would weigh their truthfulness, but not for long. Of the goyim, we only really trusted Franklin Delano Roosevelt, and he didn't come to the Aperion Plaza. "It's how afraid they are of losing next time that I watch for," my father would say of the candidates. "When you figure out who is the most afraid, you know whose promises you can take seriously."

I can't remember any of the politicians having spoken from notes. Nearly all of them Irish, they came from a tradition that equated manliness with the ability to improvise on matters of state with such sweet thunder that the crowd would be just as enchanted as if they were hearing "The Wild Colonial Boy."

For decades, one of these political nightingales easily, contemptuously, surpassed all the rest. A cunning poet, a storyteller of uncommon fire and tenderness, he glowed with an unquenchable hatred of the Boston Brahmins, a hatred that united and warmed all the immigrants of the

James Michael Curley, mayor of Boston, at his desk in City Hall, 1931; his voice, like Buddy Bolden's horn, could call in the voters from all the wards. Courtesy of Boston Public Library Print Department

Dr. Carl S. Ell, President of Northeastern University when I was a student there and my nemesis while I was editor-in-chief of the Northeastern News. Courtesy of Northeastern University Libraries, Archives and Special Collections

city — Jews, Irish, Italians, Poles, Portuguese. The grand man's name was James Michael Curley.

I heard him often when I was a boy; and when I worked in radio in my late teens and twenties, I often introduced James Michael Curley, with some awe, to his eagerly awaiting audiences from South Boston to Roxbury to the bristling Brahmins behind closed doors in their counting houses on State Street and their fine residences on Louisburg Square.

In his long and mischievous time as one of the last of the big city bosses, Curley had often been mayor of Boston (his first term began in 1914; he returned to City Hall in 1922, again in 1930, and began his fourth term in 1945). He had also often been defeated for mayor, more often than he was elected.

Curley had been a congressman too, and, from 1935 to 1936, governor of the Commonwealth of Massachusetts. Ever after, this having been the highest office he ever attained, Curley was addressed by his retainers, admirers, and those citizens who wanted a boon of him as "Governor." I called him that too, because I liked him. The Governor, by the way, had also spent some time in the slammer for criminal conspiracy to commit mail fraud. He had been in residence, as he put it, at "the University of Danbury," a federal penitentiary. Curley, by the way, was elected mayor in 1945 even though he was under indictment at the time for conspiracy to commit mail fraud. After he was convicted and sentenced to a term of six to eighteen months in Danbury, 172,000 Bostonians signed, in less than a week, a petition for leniency. Curley served five months before President Harry Truman commuted his sentence. Curley then returned to being mayor of Boston, reporting with some relish that all the Ivy League colleges had been represented in the prison yard. Certainly including Harvard.

James Michael Curley had the look of a man who was accustomed to being amused. He had a vulpine face — not the face of a mean fox but rather that of a kind and wily one who was merciless to his enemies. At some moments he looked very much like W. C. Fields closely holding a pair of deuces with which he was going to take the whole pot from the faint-at-heart at the table. His voice, which alone won him hundreds of thousands of votes over the decades, was a continual astonishment. It was a vintage pipe organ and, like Buddy Bolden's horn, could call in the voters from all the wards.

There was so much music in that voice: in the melodic flow of the phrasing; in the point-counterpoint of the themes and indignations; in the rhythms of the prophecies, sometimes swelling into a huge breaking wave against all the satanic forces focused, perpetually, on James Michael Curley. What satanic forces? Why, start with the bankers. The State Street bankers. The Brahmin bankers.

Curley was seen by many of his lifelong admirers as a sort of Robin Hood. The son of a hod carrier, Curley, it was said as regularly as the seasons, never forgot where he came from and so always kept in mind those most in need. Some of his admirers also conceded, with a wink, that certain of Curley's associates through the years benefited rather handsomely from government contracts. And that Curley himself might have received a token or two of appreciation from a contractor or two. My father, who voted for Curley more than once, never drove us through the tunnel from Logan Airport to the city without praying as we went under the water. That tunnel had been built during one of the administrations of James Michael Curley, and my father was profoundly suspicious of the quality of the contractors and of the materials they had put into the tunnel.

Curley was aware that few people in Boston, on taking a free-association test, would have instantly linked him with invincible honesty. And so it was that on a historic evening in Ward 14, Dorchester, which was almost entirely Jewish then, James Michael Curley stood in front of the G & G Delicatessen, the agora of the community, and looked down on thousands upon thousands of Jews stretching in all directions before him. "I know," James Michael Curley said, "I know people think I'm a gonif. But" — he winked at the multitude — "I don't keep it all for myself." Timpani rolls of laughter, with Curley beaming in the Jewish sky. He carried the ward handsomely.

There were intricate feuds among the Irish politicians, and at times Curley was supported by none of them for whatever office he was pursuing. During one of those campaigns, I was sitting in a meeting hall waiting for Robin Hood. I noticed that a heroic oil painting of him had been placed on the wall in back of the speaker's lectern. Already sitting onstage was an array of public servants of the people, all Irish, all of the opinion that the very best thing that could happen to the city of Boston would be for James Michael Curley to be drawn and quartered. At least twice, to make sure it took.

In came Curley, smiling, gliding up the aisle, waving to friends and ancient petitioners. Hopping onto the platform as the other candidates looked stonily into the middle distance, Curley turned his back on the other politicians and on the audience and addressed his portrait on the back wall.

"What are they doing to you, Jim?" he began. And then, in cadences more of sorrow than of anger, Curley tolled the names of the stone faces on the dais, one by one. As he came to each name, Curley, speaking to the portrait, reminded himself how he had started each one in service to the people, how each had kept rising with Curley's help, how each had betrayed the people and Jim Curley (same thing), and how each now had the incredible gall to present himself in this hall before the very people whose trust he had sold for the king's shilling.

Oh, it was not these whited sepulchers' betrayal of himself that grieved him. "We're used to that, aren't we, Jim?" Curley said, nodding sadly and familiarly to his portrait. It was what they had done to these decent, honest, working people. And here they were, panting to do it again.

Curley turned around, looking directly at the audience. "Michael, Michael, how's the wife? And how is young James, whom I was so pleased to recommend for that job with the Board of Education? And Mrs. Flannery, how good you look! The coal coming in all right? You sure now?" And on it went. Curley hadn't seeded the audience. He didn't have to. He knew that most of those who would come to such an evening would have one reason or another to remember him personally. And he surely remembered each of them. He always remembered them.

James Michael Curley had a home in Jamaicaway. As a boy going to Boston Latin School early in the morning, I would see lines of people standing on the side of the portico, waiting to see Curley before he went to the work of governing us all. As a young man, whenever I rode or walked by, I saw the same scene. Some were asking for help concerning a long-urgent complaint stuck deep in the bowels of the bureaucracy. Others needed a job referral for a son or a husband long out of work. A few simply wanted to say "Good morning and good luck," so they could hurry home or to a bar and show the hand that shook Curley's. And a goodly number were there to take, with great thanks, a couple of dollars or a fin. No questions asked. All those people, through all those years, remembered Curley. As they did at one of the lowest points in Curley's history. After he had been in public life for forty years, he found himself out of office, without a job. One of his children had just died, and he had been ordered by a court to pay a judgment of $42,629 at $500 a week. (The money was to be repaid to the City of Boston because Curley, while mayor, had taken it as payment for settling a suit against the city.)

As his biographer, Joseph Dinneen, wrote in *The Purple Shamrock:* "Curley did not have $42,629. It is doubtful that he had $42. The court sent forth investigators to find the pots of gold Curley, as nearly everyone believed, had secretly stashed through the years."

No money could be found. And Curley had to get up the $500 a week, the court said in his last appearance before it, or go to jail. On the morning after that court appearance, Dinneen wrote,

> two lines began to form outside his house on Jamaicaway, each one small and unimportant at first, alternately growing and shrinking in size as the morning wore on. Trucks, limousines, pushcarts, delivery wagons, automobiles of all sizes, shapes, makes and models were pulling up to the door, a leaderless, unorganized army of the grateful coming to his rescue. When they were questioned by reporters, they had little to say, except for occasional variations of the response: "Well, I read in the papers that the guy's behind the eight-ball. I figured he could use some dough, so I thought I'd drop by and help him out."
>
> The demonstration was spontaneous. It could not have been organized. There had not been time to organize it. No one had been aware of it until it was discovered. . . . In this line, day after day and in substantial numbers for a week or more, were the Boston Irish, the Boston Italians, Jews, Chinese, Poles, Lithuanians, a complete cross section of the city, storekeepers, merchants, contractors, city employees, filling-station owners and attendants, laundry-truck drivers, messengers, office boys, firemen, policemen, waiters, a large number of doctors and registered nurses, elevator operators, almost every trade and profession, coming into his breakfast room or library to hand over bills, change, checks, and even nickels, dimes and quarters in rolls.

All told, about fifteen hundred citizens came by the house on the Jamaicaway and gave him enough money to meet his $500-a-week obligation for at least the next six months.

got to know James Michael Curley somewhat at WMEX, the radio station where he made most of his campaign talks. As a staff announcer, all I had to do was introduce the Governor and give him time signals toward the end of his quarter hour. Curley never read from notes. He was like a jazz musician who could improvise precisely as many choruses as were needed for the occasion. The only time he ran over, or tried to, was during an especially ferocious primary campaign for mayor. Toward the end of his quarter hour one evening, Curley thought of a new and lethal line of attack on his opponent and was rollicking along when I gave him the one-minute cutoff sign. Instantly, without dropping a word, he started hauling twenty-dollar bills out of his vest pocket. As I kept shaking my head, more bills were being tossed at me. I was mouthing "FCC, FCC," and Curley kept tossing me those twenty-dollar bills.

Seeing that I was making no move to pick up the money, Curley quickly but smoothly signed off, as if that was exactly the moment at which he had intended to finish. He then picked up the bills and put them back in his pocket. Curley showed no anger at me. The bribe had been worth a try, and it hadn't worked.

During most of his campaigns, Curley not only broadcast in the evening but also bought a quarter hour each noon to serenade the ladies at home. On these broadcasts,

Curley would read poetry — no one in politics could make words sing as rapturously as Curley. And in between the poems, he would gently speak about various issues of the day, each of which could be resolved, in ways that would strengthen the family, only by James Michael Curley.

A few minutes before noon one morning at WMEX, in the corridor outside the main studio, Curley was standing with one of his advisors, Francis Kelly, who later became attorney general of Massachusetts. Kelly was what you might call a defensive thinker. He continually looked and listened ahead to see what dangers might be coming around the bend.

"What are you reading this morning, Governor?" Kelly asked.

" 'The quality of mercy is not strained,' " said Curley.

"Oh, no. Oh, no," Kelly said. "The Jews won't like that at all."

Curley thought and then nodded. "You're right, Frank. No *Merchant of Venice*. I'll give them some James Whitcomb Riley." And so he did. That morning the ladies in radioland were not the only ones for whom time stopped a few minutes later. At five past noon I looked into the control room, and the engineer was gazing raptly at the Governor, as was Francis Kelly through the window in the corridor. And Curley himself looked as if he were in a state of grace. Autointoxication, I thought. He really sees himself as his worshipers do. But years after, I read the Gaelic proverb that he used as the epigraph for his autobiography, *I'd Do It Again!*

"If the best man's faults were written on his forehead, it would make him pull his hat over his eyes."

Whatever flaws he did admit to, Curley, I came to see, regarded himself as continually redeemed by having the warmest of hearts. And when there was need, he also had blessedly quick legs to go along with the warmest of hearts. For a politician.

In *Honey Fitz*, John Henry Cutler's biography of Jack Kennedy's grandfather John F. Fitzgerald—a powerful and tumultuous figure in Boston politics for many years—there is a description of James Michael Curley walking out of City Hall in 1949 for the last time, having been defeated for reelection. Curley "slowly descended the steps of City Hall," Cutler wrote, and "when a woman deputy sheriff tried to serve a summons on him, resulting from a suit that followed his issuance of licenses to two drive-in theaters, James Michael Curley did not walk faster. Rather, he sprinted down four flights of stairs and outran the sheriff in a zany race to his car."

I voted for Curley in that election, as I had before. I knew his faults, as did everyone in Boston who read the newspapers. But there was more to him than knavery and more to him than the gusto and wit with which he governed. Oddly, the value of this other Curley was best defined by the *Boston Herald*, his most continually outraged enemy through the decades. That paper of the Brahmins nonetheless said of the rise of Curley from councilman to mayor to governor: "In his elevation, every little person was elevated. The barber in South Boston, the North End fruit dealer, the carpenter, the waiter and the school janitor— these found Boston theirs when Mr. Curley made the city his, and they could look at a State Street banker with level eye and enjoy the agony of the Brahmins. The mighty had been humbled and the yoke of inferiority lifted from the downtrodden, and what a sensation that is!"

A good many Jews also found Boston theirs when Mr. Curley made the city his. Not only the Jews he appointed to office. The rest of us knew that if there was one group for whom the Brahmins had more contempt than they had for the Irish, it was the Jews. At least the Irish were Christians, after their popish fashion. So when Curley went up against the Brahmins, as he regularly and exuberantly did, we Jews cheered him on. The Irish couldn't get into their clubs, and the Jews couldn't, but because of Curley the Brahmins couldn't get into City Hall.

It was also impossible for me not to be fond of a man who, in 1936, while being jeered by students at Williams College, told the young scholars with a small, wicked smile: "You young gentlemen should be proud of a leader like Franklin Delano Roosevelt. Consider all the fine federal prisons he has erected to house your embezzling bank-president fathers."

When he left — or, rather, sprinted — from City Hall for the last time, the *Boston Herald,* in an editorial, told of the kind of help Curley had given through the years to citizens who never got into the newspapers: "A job with the city or a contractor for the father laid off at the plant. A bed and care at City Hospital for the exhausted mother. A warning to a hounding creditor to lay off. Or just the re-assurance of a friend in power. Unless you have been poor and forlorn in a big city, you have no conception of what this means."

During his last years (he died in 1958 at the age of eighty-four), I would sometimes see Curley partaking of the public transportation system. The large, motley retinue of retainers and officeholders that had invariably accompanied him to the radio station when I worked there were gone. He would be riding alone, reading or looking at the ads in the car. And he would smile on being recognized, which, of course, he very often was.

One afternoon, Edwin O'Connor, the author of *The Last Hurrah*, walked into an MTA car and saw the Governor. O'Connor hesitated to speak to him because Curley had filed a libel suit against him and his publisher, as well as the movie company that planned to make a film of the novel. Curley contended that people identified the Irish politician Frank Skeffington, the novel's main character, with himself. But he was not Skeffington, said Curley. Skeffington was a rogue. He had nothing to do with Curley. Therefore, Curley had been defamed.

In the novel, Skeffington, on his deathbed, has given no signs of life for some time. Among others standing by the bed is one of his old enemies, a renowned whited sepulcher, who says: "I think we can say this: that knowing what he knows now, if he had it to do all over again there's not the slightest doubt but that he'd do it all very, very differently!"

At that point, O'Connor wrote, "The figure on the bed stirred . . . Skeffington had raised himself slightly. His eyes were now wide open, and in them they saw the old challenging, mocking gleam. And they heard his voice, as taking charge now for the last time, he gave his answer: "*The hell I would!*""

Standing in the public car, O'Connor was still debating whether to go over and talk to the Governor when Curley motioned to the novelist to sit down beside him. "You know," Curley said melodiously, "the part of your book I liked the best was when I was dying."

A particularly vivid figure in *The Last Hurrah* is named Charlie Hennessy. While many readers recognized Frank Skeffington as James Michael Curley, only Boston readers of the novel were likely to know that Charlie Hennessy was actually Clem Norton, for many years an unsuccessful political opponent and bemused admirer of James Michael Curley.

Hennessy enters the novel, "a short, stout man with oddly protuberant eyes . . . dressed in a rumpled grey suit . . . there was something about him which suggested perpetual and hectic movement; one felt to see him thus at a standstill was like seeing a hummingbird forcibly immobilized. It was somehow unfair."

Bustling about the streets of Boston, Clem Norton used to say, "Why, I've a million things to do — a million." Every fifteen minutes, his wristwatch alarm went off. He needed the reminder, he said, to keep his conversations short. But if he was into one of his stories, the alarm was simply not heard.

A story Clem Norton especially liked to tell about Curley was recalled by William A. Davis in his obituary of Norton in the *Boston Globe* in 1979. Curley had a habit "of cruising in his official car through the South End with a pocketful of silver dollars. Spotting some poor old woman on the sidewalk, he would stop the car, step from the limousine and intone: 'Every woman should have two things, my dear lady, beauty and money. Beauty you already had, and now you have money too'—and he would hand her a silver dollar."

Clem Norton, who did not think that Curley was nearly as intellectually imaginative, and certainly not as well read in so many disciplines as Norton himself, was often moved to say, however, that "Curley was the kindest politician I ever knew. He was always doing things like that—and he died broke."

When Norton died at eighty-four on August 11, 1979, he died full of information. His parents, who had come to Boston from Ireland, could not read, write, or tell time. But Clem stopped reading only to talk. And in his early years—working days and going to classes by night—he stopped talking long enough to take the exams that earned him college degrees in law, business, education, and the arts. He held various municipal positions, notably the chairmanship of the Boston School Committee. It was in that role that I, during my time in radio, came to know Clem Norton.

The chairman appeared once a week to tell the people of Boston what they ought to know about education—from the most ancient of times to the present progress of the scholars in the public schools of the city. Like James Michael Curley, Norton did not use a prepared text or any notes. Why, he could talk all night, and then some, simply by associating all the facts already in his head with the new shipments that were arriving every hour.

"I've read thousands of books, thousands of them!" Clem would tell me and anybody else who happened to be at the radio station. He was not so much boasting as marveling that everybody didn't walk around with a book in his hand instead of looking about aimlessly, like a cow.

Until I started talking to Clem Norton — conversations punctuated regularly by his saying in his quick lilt, "Do you follow me now?" — I had considered myself a passionate reader. I read while I spun recordings on the air, I read during the Rosary that we broadcast every evening, I read during meals, and a woman friend had once accused me of reading at a time when we were supposed to be doing something entirely together.

By contrast with Clem Norton, however, I felt that I had been wasting far too much other time when I could have been reading, and it was then I started reading on the street and carrying a small flashlight for the onset of darkness. For some forty years I have been a walking reader, hoping to come across Clem Norton somewhere to thank him for adding so much useful time to my years.

Clem never married. The public life was all he wanted — that and time by himself in the Athenaeum, the Widener Library at Harvard, and especially the Boston Public Library at Copley Square, where for half a century he had his own corner where he did his research and his writing.

For much of his life he was superintendent of the Commonwealth Pier and happy enough in that work, except for one continually elusive dream. Clem wanted to be mayor of Boston, and for nearly thirty years he tried often, failing each time.

It may be that he thought too fast and talked too fast

for the voters. And he probably irritated the citizenry because he was always after them to take better care of themselves and their children. Clem enthusiastically kept up with all the new discoveries about the pleasures of food, drink, and sloth that led to shortened lives.

As Frank Skeffington said of Charlie Hennessy in *The Last Hurrah:* "He's a good fellow, smart enough and knows the political situation from A to Z, and as I say, he won't take a dime from anybody. [But] Charlie's not content with asking the voters to lend him their ears; halfway through the speech he starts wanting to take their pulse, as well."

I always looked forward to Clem Norton bouncing up the stairs with two minutes to go before airtime, depositing his armful of magazines and newspapers on a couch outside the studio and breezing in just in time to tell the radio audience of some of the astonishing things he'd learned about all kinds of subjects since he last clued them in to the wonders and dangers around them.

And afterwards, he would show me a magazine I had never heard of before and then tell me about a cute trick James Michael Curley had played on the State Street bankers the day before yesterday. Hopping in place, his eyes bright, his voice gliding, Clem would suddenly stop. "Do you follow me now?"

When he died, they named a city playground after him. Clem would have liked that — particularly if the public library put a bookmobile in it.

Clem Norton once asked me where I had gone to college. Northeastern, I said.

"Well," he said. "They don't let you waste your time there." That was true in more ways than he knew.

I had not intended by any means to go to Northeastern, which was regarded at the time as a place for children of the working class. Non-Jewish children of the working class. Jewish students of whatever class were expected, if they were college material, to attend Harvard or Yale or Tufts or, if they had slept through high school, Boston University. But not cheerless, sooty Northeastern, which didn't even have a tree, let alone a campus.

While at Boston Latin School, I had been afflicted with a rare mental disorder. I had decided I wanted to major in Greek in college and that the only fit place for this passionate pursuit was among the Jesuits at Boston College. Although I had taken three years of Greek at Latin School, Mr. Winslow, a venerable, vaguely kind member of the faculty from Maine, did not count me among his small crop of true scholars. Indeed, what I had most often heard from him during those three years was, "Ingenious, Mr. Hentoff, but wrong."

Maybe it was a biochemical imbalance that propelled me not only to apply to Boston College but to make it my only choice. Although I had managed to grow up un-

At age fifteen, with my sister, Janet, in 1940.
Courtesy of Janet Krauss

As a student at Northeastern
University in 1941.
Courtesy of Janet Krauss

maimed in the most anti-Semitic city in the nation, it never occurred to me when I applied that there might be a Jewish quota in this Catholic college. There was, of course, reasonably enough. I didn't make the cut.

The crushing news from the Jesuits came after all the other desirable colleges had made their selections. And most of the undesirable ones as well. I was in such a state of panic that even Billie Holiday recordings couldn't settle me down. I was going to be the only member of my class who would not be in college in September. The neighborhood would be whispering behind my parents' backs, pointing fingers, saying with lip-smacking pleasure, "That's what happens to a boy who sits on the porch on Yom Kippur and eats a salami sandwich so that everyone on the way to shul should see him. You think God doesn't write such things down?"

My parents couldn't be of any help, for they knew nothing of colleges or applications. They did want to know why their son had applied to only one college, and why he had wanted to major in Greek there. I snapped at them that they certainly weren't being of any use asking such questions.

At last it occurred to me that there was only one college that might take me so late in the game. Northeastern, on Huntington Avenue, near Symphony Hall, had been in existence since 1898, and while it had acquired some reputation as an engineering school, its other divisions — particularly a rather scrawny liberal arts section — were hardly renowned or recommended in Boston or anywhere else. The admissions office, I hoped, might look kindly on me as probably the first Boston Latin School graduate to knock on Northeastern's door, and since there was never an excess of liberal arts applicants anyway, I might be able to avoid the abiding shame, in my ghetto, of being just a high school graduate.

I was accepted with such alacrity that I thought my life was ruined. Clearly, Northeastern would accept anybody at all.

Northeastern University turned out to be a more serious place of learning than I had thought. That is, I learned a lot more from the other students than I had at Boston Latin School. Not only were they of the working class, but many actually had grown-up jobs. A cop had the locker next to mine; and a couple of years later, when women were let in, I sometimes walked to class with a former organizer for the United Mine Workers, who was now inventing remarkably resourceful tales of adultery and marijuana abuse for *True Story* in order to support herself and her young daughter, and pay her tuition. Also in my class were a jazz musician and an apprentice reporter at the *Boston Globe*.

Nearly all of us were the first members of our families to go to college. There was no way we could have allowed ourselves to drop out, because that would have meant our whole families would be dropping out.

At Latin School, although I'd had friends, I was essentially an outsider. Most of the boys were in such fierce, constant competition with each other for grades and for the very best places in the world to come that they weren't interested in talking about anything else. At Northeastern, however, while everyone studied hard, we also read the papers, including the funnies; jawed about James Michael Curley and FDR; were curious — at least in the liberal arts division — about Marxism; and sang Gilbert and Sullivan, backwards as well as forwards, in the common room. The course loads were heavy; all of us commuted; and yet there seemed to be a lot of time for fun. A strange word for a Jewish boy to associate with school.

It was clear that the most fun was in the offices of the *Northeastern News*. As a freshman passing by those offices, yearning to join the rebels, I gathered the courage to apply for a tryout. I worked very hard on my first piece, a straight news story, and proudly presented it, neatly written, to the managing editor. He looked at the manuscript, guffawed in a most demeaning way, showed it to several other braying staff members, and pointed to a typewriter. That day, I learned how to type.

The *Northeastern News* consisted of a large main room and the inner office of the editor-in-chief. In the latter space, there was a sempiternal blackjack game, starting soon after seven in the morning (Northeastern awoke with the sun) and lasting until nine or ten at night (Northeastern needed little sleep). The game was suspended only on Monday nights, when the paper was made up. The stakes were not high, but since the gaming hours were so long, a particularly skillful player could go home with an added fifty dollars or so in his kick. There were two sharp-eyed majors in sociology who, over four years, took care of most of their tuition payments from their winnings. They might have decided to spend the rest of their lives in the inner offices of the *Northeastern News,* had they not discovered girls when the university went coed.

One editor-in-chief, a small, icy divinity student, was even more consumed by blackjack fever than the rest of us were. He left the inner office only to attend the minimum number of classes to keep himself in school, and he mostly concerned himself with the running of the paper when editorials were due, and they were very brief. The rest of the time he would stand behind his desk, praying for a ten and a picture card.

The doors to both the outer room and the inner office were kept closed because of a university regulation subjecting anyone who gambled for money on Northeastern's premises to banishment for an indefinite period. We knew that the president of Northeastern, Carl S. Ell, was a man of his cold word. His only passion was the university, and clemency toward anyone who had sullied it was as foreign to his nature as a trip to the Old Howard Burlesque Show.

One careless evening, however, the doors to both the main and the inner office had been left open. The divinity student, standing behind his desk, an ace of clubs in his hand, was just about to turn over a card on the table when the Reverend Charles Havice, dean of chapel and conductor of such courses as "God and the Nature of Evil," came through the door. Dean Havice was a man of such ceaseless amiability that in some circles he was suspected of not having all his marbles. But at that moment he looked at the divinity student with a decidedly pained, betrayed look.

The divinity student finished uncovering a ten, slammed the ace on top of it, and said to Dean Havice, with the utmost seriousness, "Sir, as you have so often told us, one has to sin before he can repent."

The dean looked sorrowfully at the divinity student, at each of us, turned around, and left. So far as we knew, he did not report us to President Ell. And he himself never mentioned the incident to any of us.

"Charlie is a true Christian," said the divinity student. "He would not deliver us to the Philistines. But keep the goddamn doors locked from now on."

Despite the nearly nonstop gambling, we got the paper out on time, and it was even readable. It may be that the crisp sound of the cards hitting the desk in the inner office served as a seductive invitation to those of us at our typewriters outside to keep our stories short.

For the first two years I was on staff, the paper concentrated almost entirely on university news; but in my third year, I was elected editor-in-chief by the staff, and the *Northeastern News* took the world as its beat. Well, primarily that part of the world that was Boston.

Our model was the New York daily *PM*, a boisterously muckraking engine of irreverence which was so unbeholden to any commercial interests that it accepted no advertising. It was a paper of the left but, we felt, insufficiently anti-Communist, so we handled our own foreign policy. (My second-in-command, a sometime union organizer, also tended to give the best assignments, however local, to reporters who were duly reverent of *Darkness at Noon*.)

What we liked about *PM* was its chortling delight in breaking stories that none of the other dailies in New York had heard of (or had pretended not to have heard of). We tried to do much the same in Boston, tracking down, for example, the bankrollers of some of the city's anti-Semitic sects and their publications.

At the plant that printed the *Northeastern News,* we found a cache of anti-Semitic sheets, and we went on from that lead. We also contacted several Jewish organizations in Boston, expecting they would help us spread the news about these traffickers in anti-Semitism. They did no such thing. They tried to get us to kill the story. Just as Jewish community leaders had tried to keep the news of violence against Jews in Roxbury and Dorchester out of the papers — by direct contrast to Fran Sweeney's insistence that anti-Semitism, in all its forms, be exposed. Continually.

At the time, I didn't write about their trying to convince us to censor ourselves. But forty years later, when most of the major Jewish organizations in Boston were again silent, refusing this time to protect a young woman from an anti-Semitic firestorm, I reported her story and also took public note of her abandonment by the leaders of the Jewish community, who then took indignant public note of me.

In 1944, when I went to see officials of a number of Jewish defense organizations with my leads on the financial sources for the printing and distribution of certain anti-Semitic publications in Boston, I was not met with the keen interest I had expected.

Their advice was *"Sha!"* — quiet. To print such stories

is not good for the Jews, I was told. They only encourage other anti-Semites to go and do likewise. So we gave the story to *PM*, which came into town, shaming the Boston dailies into gingerly poking at the story. In the *Northeastern News*, I didn't write about the timid Jewish officials because I couldn't bring myself to expose them in public in a paper read mostly by non-Jews, even if I was the editor of that paper. But I was angry at them, and I was angry at myself for not having denounced them.

In the fall of 1984 Susan Shapiro, a high-school senior in Randolph, Massachusetts, gave me a second chance.

The seventeen-year-old had refused to stand for the morning ritual of singing the national anthem and pledging allegiance to the flag. During her junior year she had also preferred not to join the loyalty rites, but her teacher then had left that decision to each member of the class. He did not believe that ceremonial loyalty could be or should be forced.

But Mrs. Jean Noblin, Susan's homeroom teacher for her last year at Randolph High School, had decidedly different views. The first time Susan refused to stand, Mrs. Noblin told her to snap to, and Susan did.

The next day, however, Susan brought to school a pamphlet published by the United States Government, "Your Legal Rights and Responsibilities — for Public School Students." It told students: "You may not be forced to take part in the salute to the flag or Pledge of Allegiance if doing so violates your beliefs or values."

Mrs. Noblin was not impressed. In her twenty-nine years of teaching at Randolph High School, no student — until now — had refused to show respect for this nation and what it stood for. So when seventeen-year-old Susan Shapiro told her that the flag was only a symbol, a piece of cloth, and that it didn't make sense to her to stand up for a symbol, Mrs. Noblin answered sharply that the cross is a symbol, and the Star of David is a symbol, and how would Susan like it if someone were to spit on the Star of David?

Susan, as she told me, took this last comment as an unduly pointed reference to the fact that her last name is Shapiro.

The teacher sent the young woman of dubious patriotism to the principal's office. The principal knew, if Mrs. Noblin did not, that the Supreme Court had spoken on this matter in a 1943 case involving children of Jehovah's Witnesses, who would not salute the flag because the Old Testament forbids bowing to any image. Those children had been expelled from school, but the Supreme Court sent them back, saying that "compulsory unification of opinion achieves only the unanimity of the graveyard."

Susan Shapiro, therefore, went back to her homeroom without penalty. Her teacher, however, was not in the least admonished for having been disrespectful of Susan's First Amendment rights in this matter.

None of this would have gone beyond conversations at Randolph dinner tables and gas stations if the press had not taken up the story — first the local papers, then the wire services, national television, and the *New York Times*.

Once it became widely known that this Jewish girl was spitting on the flag — Mrs. Noblin's helpful illustration gained wide currency — many decidedly unpleasant letters and phone calls were received by the Shapiro family. Among the messages:

"Dirty Jew bastards, too bad *you* weren't put in the ovens."

"It *can* happen here! Think about it—Jew!"

"You fucking Jewish whore. Only people like you and your kind would do something like this and dishonor the flag. You don't belong here—why don't you get out of here and go back to Israel."

The only difference between those expressions of warm regard and the anti-Semitic handbills of my boyhood was that there was no Israel then. In those years, we were told to go back to Russia—with whose government we were probably in covert contact anyway.

The Shapiro family also picked up a number of death threats, including:

"Because Hitler didn't finish the job right, we are going to."

And a Ku Klux Klan affiliate in Texas promised to pay a visit to the Shapiros that would be the last visit the family would ever have.

The Justice Department became involved to ensure Susan's safety in school, and the office of the Massachusetts attorney general investigated the death threats. The thrust of sentiment in the Shapiros' hometown was indicated by Gerald Rumbos, commander of the Randolph chapter of the Veterans of Foreign Wars: "You can do anything you want in this country, but if you don't stand up for the flag, you don't belong in this country."

At the high school, I found out, the faculty vehemently declared themselves on the side of Mrs. Jean Noblin, and the great majority of the students either coldly ignored Susan or made it plain to her that she was a disgrace to the school and to the nation. Some of the kids brought little American flags to school to make sure Susan didn't miss the point.

Late one Saturday night, in the darkness behind the Shapiros' home, a group of kids from the high school serenaded the family with a sardonic rendering of "The Star-Spangled Banner."

Outside the high school, while a surge of anti-Semitism was to be expected after it became national knowledge that a Shapiro had not shown respect to the American flag, the utter passivity of the major Jewish organizations in the Boston-Randolph area was quite startling. (The Anti-Defamation League had shown a brief interest in the venomous attention being paid to the Shapiros, but then it joined the silence of the other Jewish groups.)

So remarkable was this abandonment of the Shapiros by all the organizations which initially came into being because Jews were vulnerable that the *Jewish Advocate* in Boston — a paper I had been reading since childhood — said in a lead editorial, "Don't Tread on Susan," in its November 29, 1984, edition:

"The family has been shunned by the Jewish and non-Jewish communities with equal disdain. . . . Where were the voices of the traditional community organizations? . . . Was there no organization or group of individuals to issue a simple press release condemning the anti-Semitic acts against the Shapiro family?"

Said Susan Shapiro's mother, Harriet, to the *Jewish Advocate:* "The Jews in this community are afraid."

A Jewish reporter in Boston told me why the Jewish establishment found the Shapiros an embarrassment:

"First of all, they don't live in the better part of Randolph, where most of the Jewish community is to be found. Second, the Shapiros are not only of the wrong class, they're also fighters. It's true that many of the Jews in Randolph, on both sides of town, had their origins in the working-class Jews of Roxbury and Dorchester who came out to places like Randolph in the late 1960s, when Roxbury and Dorchester stopped being Jewish communities. But the Shapiros still have the old combative spirit of those Boston Jews. They're not 'sweet.'

"People like the Shapiros cause a certain amount of uneasiness among the Jews in the right part of Randolph. There has been anti-Semitism around there before, and the fear is that Jews like the Shapiros could stir it up again for all the Jews."

Furthermore, the Shapiros did not belong to a synagogue, so why, the argument went, should they expect protection from Jews who did fulfill their communal obligations by helping support a shul?

In the *Washington Post* and in a series of articles in the *Village Voice,* I accused the Jewish "defense" organizations of egregious irrelevance in the matter of the Shapiro family. The *Boston Globe* picked up two of my pieces, with much resultant agitation in the Boston Jewish community, climaxed by a visit to the *Globe* from a delegation of Jewish leaders protesting my "destructive journalism." They then composed a letter saying the same thing that was prominently displayed in the *Globe* and signed by the chief executive officers of the Jewish Community Council, the New England Region of the American Jewish Committee, the New England Region of the Anti-Defamation League, and the New England Region of the American Jewish Congress.

In my answer, also printed in the *Globe*, I gave the sources for my charges against the official Jewish defense organizations — starting with what the Shapiros had told me. I wrote not only on behalf of the challenged fifty-nine-year-old journalist in New York, but with even more feeling for the eighteen-year-old editor of the *Northeastern News* who, forty-one years before, had been told by the predecessors of these ornaments of the Jewish establishment to cool it — indeed, to kill a story on anti-Semitism.

The public debate between me and the official Jews of Boston ended at that point. I would have been delighted if it had continued all winter and into the spring. Meanwhile, Susan Shapiro kept exemplifying what Bostonians of my youth used to call stick-to-it-iveness. For quite a while, she was shunned by most of the students at the high school. A few did speak to her — to threaten to beat her up. The consensus at school was that she had no respect for her country or for the much-beloved Jean Noblin.

A reporter for the school newspaper told the *Quincy Patriot Ledger* that his politics class had discussed the case. Many students, he said, were extremely angry and intolerant of Susan Shapiro. "It's hate, and you could feel the hate."

Susan told me: "I'm not going to let them scare me away. I want to show them I'm not afraid of them."

In the Jewish press around the country, Susan received little support, and a lot of contempt. In Florida, a woman suggested that Susan be exchanged for a Russian child who would truly appreciate freedom. *The Minneapolis-St. Paul American Jewish World* editorialized: "We dare to state that Susan Shapiro is a spoiled brat, that she proved nothing and presented herself as a vain, disrespectful youngster who sought attention with a vain deed."

And in the *Jewish Floridian,* in an editorial that could have been written forty-one years ago, associate editor Leo Mindlin wrote that "Susan Shapiro is technically correct, but I wish she hadn't done it. Because she is Jewish, the result of Shapiro's 'me' spree splatters us all in a kind of anti-Semitic counteroffensive . . ."

A self-respecting minority of letter writers did, however, understand the significance of Susan Shapiro's initial act of refusal and the resultant anti-Semitism. In the *Jewish Advocate* (January 24, 1985) Toby Liederman wrote:

"I'm frightened and sad that almost all Jews (and non-Jews) have remained silent or have condemned her for choosing a Constitutional right! And that only a handful is decrying the anti-Semitism is perhaps the most frightening of all.

"Haven't we Jews learned the awful lesson of silence? Even if you don't agree with her choice, how can you remain silent as she suffers the rage of anti-Semites? Don't you know she is you?"

The headline for the letter was WE ARE ALL SHAPIRO.

Susan had told me that had she been old enough to vote in 1984, she would have gone for Ronald Reagan. And in the spring of the next year, she told the *Jewish Advocate* that one of her heroes was Meir Kahane: "I think he's great. I like what he stands for and says."

I remembered eating the salami sandwich in plain view on Yom Kippur when I was younger than Susan, and I recognized part of myself in her.

During the furor started by Susan Shapiro's refusal to yield her First Amendment rights, something had been missing. The anti-Semites had come parading in. Jews had fought Jews on what should have been done by Jews. But where were the non-Jews?

Neither the clergy nor any elected officials in Boston or in Randolph offered Susan an ecumenical embrace as she was being attacked. But, as I should have remembered from my childhood, that too was to be expected. Susan is fortunate, however. Father Charles E. Coughlin has gone to his reward. What *he* would have made of a student named Shapiro spitting on the American flag! There would have been carloads of youngsters coming from Boston to Randolph — and not to sing in the dark.

Had the Susan Shapiro story broken in the early 1940s, we would have played it big in the *Northeastern News*. Not that we didn't occasionally break campus stories too — the overfunded athletic department, certain deficiencies in the curriculum, and the authoritarianism of President Carl S. Ell, who had never before been referred to in the campus newspaper with less than reverence.

Ell, reared in rural Indiana, had acquired a civil engineering degree from MIT and in 1910 became an instructor in engineering at the Boston Young Men's Christian Association's Evening Institute for Young Men, which was to become Northeastern. Seven years later he became dean of the engineering school and in his first year almost doubled the size of the student body. A man of ceaseless energy and bereft of all humor, Ell, who became Northeastern's second president in 1940, was in total command of every aspect of the university.

He regarded Northeastern as the sole reason for his having been put in this world. He nurtured it, disciplined it, and directed it like the true autocrat he was. He believed that no higher privilege existed anywhere than being allowed to study at, and work for, Northeastern University. As former Dean of University Administration Rudolph M. Morris says in his book *Where? On Huntington Ave.*, Dr. Ell's abiding conviction was that "the university existed for the university. Students, faculty and administration were there to serve the university."

And: "Students were there to learn and not interfere with the conduct of the institution."

No one spoke familiarly to Dr. Ell. Not even aides who had been with him for many years. And certainly not students. Always striding purposefully, Ell would march past us, a juggernaut in a dark suit, his balding head his only sign of imperfection. It was best not to catch his eye, for then he might remember you later, and Dr. Ell did not exercise his memory in order to give rewards.

I discovered indirectly that Dr. Ell had begun to express an interest in me one afternoon in the office of Harold Melvin, dean of students, for whom I worked grading the psychology tests of entering freshmen and doing other office chores. His secretary, Mary Craig, was an object of exotic fascination for me. I had known a few shiksas but, except for Frances Sweeney, only fleetingly. This was the first one I talked with regularly, casually, and, in time, in easily flowing friendship. She came from a family of some means in Milton, a clean, well-lit Christian suburb of Boston, and she was a graduate of Wheaton College. Mary was not going to be a secretary forever. She was going to get married. Blond, merry, generous, a fount of gossip, sharply and mockingly observant, Mary was a grand prize. But not for a Jewish boy.

I was of some exotic interest to her. Growing up, she had known no Jews and had had few Jewish acquaintances at Wheaton. So Mary was curious. What was this kosher stuff we ate? And this ritual bath? What did the women *do* in this ritual bath? Now don't misunderstand this question, Nat, but how come you people are always buying things wholesale? And why are you all so smart? Is it genetic, or maybe diet?

On the afternoon Dr. Ell's name came up, I was filing a batch of grades when Mary, looking again to see that Dr. Melvin's office was empty, whispered, "They want to throw you out."

That morning, she had heard several very high-level administrators tell Dean Melvin that Dr. Ell had had enough of my troublemaking with the newspaper. The final straw had been those calls to the trustees.

"What calls?" Mary asked.

"We're going to do a series," I said, "on the board of trustees. Why are they on the board? Because they know anything about education, or because they give a lot of money?"

Mary shook her head. "You know what your problem

is? You just want to call attention to yourself all the time. Well, Buster, you certainly have done it this time. They told Dean Melvin they want all your records, and then they'll figure out how to get rid of you."

Dean Melvin was a man of generous spirit and a passionate and true scholar. He had taught Shakespeare for some thirty years, and yet each semester he would begin his lecture as if he had just come from the Globe Theatre. I was not surprised when Mary told me that Dean Melvin had tried to resist handing over my records, but the order had come from the president, and Melvin had been at Northeastern too long not to know what happened to field officers who disobeyed a command, even distinguished scholars.

"The dean is very upset," Mary told me. "He'd like to talk to you about this, but he can't because it's secret."

The next day, when the dean had left his office, Mary beckoned me to her desk. "They're not going to kick you out." She smiled. "They didn't realize you had a 4.0 average. I mean, how do you kick out somebody with all A's? And there's nothing bad on your record. Except for being a troublemaker, you're a good boy. So they're going to kick you off the newspaper."

"They'll have to bring charges," I said.

"No, they don't, dummy. They'll give you a choice."

That's exactly what happened. The other editors and I were summoned to the office of William C. White, second-in-command to President Ell. A tall, broad-shouldered man with an easy manner and a somewhat too ready smile, White motioned us to chairs and said that the university had adopted a new policy concerning the *Northeastern*

News. The paper was to confine its reporting and commentary to the affairs of the university. Period. There were to be no exceptions. All editors would have to sign an agreement to abide by this new policy.

White gave each of us a copy of the agreement. "There must be no misunderstanding—" He looked at me. "For instance, any reporting on the members of the board of trustees will be limited to their decisions concerning this university, not to anything else about them."

Each of us looked at the agreement and then at each other. "Tell President Ell," I said to White, "that he has my resignation." The other editors also handed the unsigned sheets to White. I never knew what White himself thought of being the conduit for the offer Carl Ell knew I would have to refuse. White was just doing his job.

On the way back to clean out our desks and pack the decks of cards away, we felt positively buoyant in our virtue. We had not sold out to retain office. Our resignations were an act of defiance of the deity of the place, and we were still alive. It took a couple of days for the deep blues to set in, and some of us never quite stopped mourning our loss of the paper.

Predictably, a scab was found on the reporting staff, and he took over as editor of the *Northeastern News*. Our board of exiles could barely wait to take the paper apart every week.

In my senior year I was awarded the President's Letter. Based entirely on academic records, it was the highest honor a Northeastern undergraduate could attain. Having kept up my 4.0 average, I had to be given the award because no one else had all A's. The President's Letter was just that, I was disappointed to find out. No check. Just a letter from

Dr. Ell saying how pleased he and Northeastern had been to have me. But there was a dinner for the winner at which President Ell, from time immemorial, had presented the letter.

"Dr. Ell is not coming," said Mary Craig.

"He's got to come," I said. "It's *his* letter."

"He won't. He won't give you the satisfaction. Dr. Lynd from the government department will present you with the letter."

The night I was awarded the President's Letter, there were a number of toasts, all of them irreverent, but Dr. Ell's name was never mentioned. I think we felt some sorrow for the autocrat of Huntington Avenue. For the first time in his long reign, he had placed himself in the bizarre and indeed humiliating position of boycotting himself, for he *was* the university and all its functions, especially those that bore his name.

We were even. Dr. Ell had forced me to give up something I prized; and by winning the President's Letter, I had forced him to publicly cut off his nose to spite his face. But if we were even, why did I still feel so angry at him?

My obsession with the First Amendment is due to Carl S. Ell. James Madison came later. Ell's way of arranging my self-removal from the *Northeastern News* was not a First Amendment matter. Northeastern was a private university, so no state action was involved in the censoring of my paper. Nonetheless, the spirit of the First Amendment had been rebuked and scorned; and ever since the day of my defenestration, everyone's free-speech rights have been my business. Actually, I should be grateful to Carl S. Ell for having given me a life's work.

About twelve years later, when I was the New York editor of *Down Beat,* a reporter from the *Northeastern News* called me. The paper was doing a short feature on my jazz writing. I suggested he look at some of the jazz pieces I'd done while editing the *Northeastern News.* He called back and said that the bound volumes of my tenure were missing. He had checked around. They were not in the library, or in any other place he had searched. I did some checking of my own and was told by a not-for-attribution source in the administration that those issues had been deemed unworthy of the tradition of the *Northeastern News* and, accordingly, had been banished to some distant dungeon. "I can't prove it," my source said, "but it was Ell. He's never forgiven you for making him miss that dinner."

As N. Rubashov says to his diary in *Darkness at Noon:* "We concentrated all our efforts on preventing error and destroying the very seeds of it."

By the end of the 1960s, I was told that the bound volumes had mysteriously reappeared.

In 1973 I was asked to journey back to Huntington Avenue to accept a University Medal in recognition of my "distinguished professional achievements." At the ceremony, I told the students and faculty that my primary profession is being a troublemaker, and I had received invaluable early instruction in that calling from Frances Sweeney and at Northeastern University. I then described how zealously Dr. Ell, during my years there, had maintained Northeastern as a place of unfettered free inquiry, except when he didn't like the results of that inquiry.

Carl S. Ell was no longer Northeastern's president. His successor, Asa S. Knowles, listened to my detailed accounting with unruffled equanimity, for he had had nothing to do with those ancient events. Some of the students and the younger faculty seized on what I was saying because they were engaged in current skirmishes with the administration and could use my account to demonstrate the darker side of the Northeastern tradition.

Although Dr. Ell had retired in 1959, he still had an office at the university, and from there he kept monitoring his creation. He did not come to see me get my University Medal. Nor did he send a note. I am fond of the medal, but it is not a newspaper.

In 1985, Northeastern gave me an honorary doctorate of laws at a commencement ceremony. Dr. Ell did not attend, having died in 1981.

Not far from Northeastern's then extremely modest campus on Huntington Avenue was another institution of learning, the Savoy Café. The Savoy was at the beginning of black Boston. Except for cops, the whites who crossed over the line and into the Savoy were the jazz crazed, of almost all ages, from Boston and its environs. Some were students from Harvard, Radcliffe, MIT, and the other universities in the area, but those came intermittently, mostly on weekends and Sunday afternoons. It was not at their tables that the musicians sat. And they were not asked by the bartender-owner, Steve Connolly, for advice on whom to book. They were just fans; they weren't the regulars.

I was one of the regulars, and no membership in any organization since has meant as much to me. Nor have I ever been part of as motley a membership. There was, for instance, a huge, selectively gentle bank guard with a passion for "Muskrat Ramble" and any other tune with plenty of elbow room for a tailgate trombone. Irish, he worked in South Boston.

Another regular, German by descent, was the vice president of a bank in Milton. Milton is the kind of suburb where, if you're a black executive waiting in your car on a Sunday morning for your daughter who's been having a sleepover date with a white girlfriend, you may find yourself dragged out of your car and kneed and handcuffed by observant police. I am referring to an actual case in Milton in the early 1980s. Things were worse thirty years before. The bank vice-president was sickened by racism, and when he invited black jazzmen to his home, he made sure they weren't frisked on the lawn. He would tell the cops beforehand who was coming to dinner. The bank vice-president is dead now, but if he were still alive and still living in that pleasant town, he'd still have to alert the police in advance if he didn't want some trumpeter's lip busted. Or, as Malcolm X used to tell me with his mocking smile, "It's up South, where you folks are, that's going to hold on, and hold on."

I can't recall a single mention of Jim Crow in class at Boston Latin School. Our American history text had been printed around the time of the Spanish-American War, and among its few lyrical passages were descriptions of the antebellum South, particularly about how the air vibrated with music on the plantations — from the virginal in the parlor to the charming children's games and ring-shouts in the slave quarters. Our teacher did not dispute the text, nor did any of us, including the only black student in our class. There were, of course, no blacks on the Boston Latin School faculty.

Nor were there any black professors at Northeastern University then. I had learned very little of black American history at either school, but I was involved in a number of seminars on the subject at the Savoy. A trumpet player, originally from Florida, told me how, in a number of towns in that state, a black man had to have a pass to be on the streets at night if he didn't want to be assaulted by the police and thrown in jail. The pass had to be signed by some upstanding white citizen. Other musicians told me of other black codes where they'd grown up or where they'd lived for some time — including Boston at that very moment. I could see something of the Boston black code myself, because cops from time to time would haul black citizens into the alley next to the Savoy and interrogate them with their fists. It was understood, without the need for posting any sign, that if any onlooker protested by so much as a question, he would no longer be an onlooker.

But the Savoy Café was a sanctuary. Most of the cops were dismayed and disgusted at the "mixing" going on in the club. Especially, of course, by the sight of young white women going through the door with black men, usually black musicians. But, with very few exceptions, the police did not hassle these wanton couples. And they never swaggered in, as they did in some other black-and-white clubs, just to make everyone else anxious. It was my belief, never contradicted, that the proprietor, Steve Connolly, had provided a tidy regular annuity for the higher-ranking officers of the precinct in return for the protection of the miscegenators at the Savoy.

There did come a time, however, when *I* needed protection from a cop. But there was nothing Steve could do about my particular case. The cop was a black detective. In appearance and temperament, he had more than a faint resemblance to a rhinoceros. In and out of the precinct house, he had left a trail of mashed prisoners. White or black, it made no difference to him, although blacks who had been alone with this detective said later, not for attribution, that he was particularly vicious to his own.

But he had no "own." Not that anyone knew. Or could imagine. On the force he was a loner. Most of the force being Irish, this was by mutual preference. Although, as some of the jazz musicians whispered, even if the force had been all black, he would have been a loner. No one had ever seen him smile or heard of such a thing, even when he was working someone over in custody. Or not in custody.

Steve Connolly had hired an intermission singer-pianist, recommended by a bassist of stature. In her early twenties, from New York, she was unknown to the regulars and to the local musicians. Tall, black, shy, a merely passable pianist, she could quiet a room, even on a weekend, as soon as she began to sing. Her voice was deep, made darker by a carefully controlled vibrato, and it ranged over at least three octaves. Improvising, she glided and swooped, floated in midair, and gently, sensuously returned to earth.

The black detective became obsessed with her, but she wouldn't go out with him. He tried to scare her into affection, but that didn't work. I had become obsessed with her too, and I would sometimes walk her home. This was regarded by everyone at the Savoy, from Steve Connolly to the bouncer, as inescapable proof that the myth was wrong —not all Jews have brains.

"You want to get it over with?" the bouncer said. "Why not just put your head on the subway track?"

But someone was riding shotgun for me. Frankie Newton, a tall trumpet player, much admired for his concise lyricism, had been working in Boston for some months, and the Savoy was one of his hangouts. Newton was what used to be called a "race man." He thought black—in terms of history, politics, culture. And language.

One night a photographer to whom Newton had owed some money for a long time asked for it, again, at the bar of the Savoy. The trumpeter gave him half of what he owed.

"That's mighty white of you," the photographer grumbled.

Frankie Newton grabbed the photographer by his tie and lifted him up to eye level. "You mean that's mighty black of me," Newton whispered. Steve Connolly, who had been washing glasses at the time, later said he thought that was pretty witty.

Frankie Newton was not a separatist. He had white friends. He saw no reason to segregate himself because he thought black. You had to deal with all kinds. After all, a musician could have a beer with a club owner. Fortunately for me, I was one of Frankie's friends.

Nobody had to fill him in on what was happening. He had seen the singer shake off the detective a number of times, and he had seen the way I looked at her when she was on. And when she wasn't on.

Walking her home one night when the black detective had been seen in the neighborhood earlier, I tried to keep from turning around, because I didn't know what I would do if I saw the rhinoceros behind us. But after a few minutes I couldn't control my terror, and I turned. Half a block away was a tall, ambling black man, looking into store windows, glancing speculatively at the moon, humming a medley of Ellington tunes, and paying no attention whatever to us. All the way to the black rooming house where she stayed, Frankie Newton kept pace with us, and he did the same with me alone as I walked back to where I lived, just over the boundary line between white and black Boston. We could have walked back together, but he didn't seem to want it that way.

The next night, at the Savoy, I thanked him. "Hell," he said, "you two weren't hiding."

Before the singer left town, I walked her home a few more times, followed each time by a tall, humming black man.

For months after, I kept expecting some kind of retribution from the detective, but nothing happened. There was one night when I left the Savoy so drunk I had no memory of getting home. Sometime later, when it was still dark, I was awakened by a furious pounding on my door. Just pounding. No voice. I was seized by a desperate desire to open the door, but I couldn't get the room steady enough so that I could get up. I kept trying to rise, but I was just getting dizzier and dizzier. The pounding lasted for what seemed like a long time and then abruptly stopped. I was still trying to get to the door, but the room was moving even faster now. I gave up, fell down, and slept.

There is not the slightest evidence that my very late caller that night was the detective. After all, if it had been the rhinoceros, he could have shot the lock off or kicked the door down in hot pursuit. I was sure of only one thing. Whoever had been at that door greatly desired that night to be my last. I was saved by lack of self-control.

Whoever it was never came back, at least not so I could hear him. What troubled me almost as much as not knowing who had been behind the door was not knowing why I had been so terribly determined to get up and let him in. And would that be the case the next time, too? I still wonder about that once in a while.

Another of the regulars at the Savoy was a Dr. Pat Patten, a psychiatrist who had turned himself into an expert on tuberculosis as soon as he found out he had it. Eventually, he directed his own treatment, which was successful. Light-haired, slight, Pat spoke with the soft cadences of his native Mississippi. He had quite a range of passionate avocations — the blues, the proper care of cactus needles for playing recordings, Faulkner, comic strips, Billie Holiday, Thucydides, Dixie Belle gin, New Orleans jazz, linguistics, and spreading the news of the ineluctable end of the world, once Hiroshima had become a household word: "Historically, Nathan, it is appropriate that the end of man shall have been caused by a haberdasher rather than a king. If we must go, let us go as egalitarians."

Actually, there was little that Pat was not knowledgeable about. He cooked; he was something of a botanist; and he considered himself a masterful diagnostician. Just by the use of his eyes, anywhere he was. At the Savoy, for example, as a clarinetist left the stand, Pat would say: "Three years. Maybe five. A stroke, for sure." He saw cancer in another player. Pat kept score, and give or take a year or two, he came out pretty well.

Though I dreaded doing it for a long time, I finally asked him to look into the end of me. He didn't even turn toward me. "About fifty-five, I think — a cerebral hemorrhage. You won't know a thing. Very good way to go."

Ib, his wife, grimaced whenever Pat gave out the black spot. Except for medical diagnoses, she was just as sharp of eye and diversely knowledgeable as her husband, but it took a while to find that out, because she spoke seldom, though unfailingly to the point. Like Frances Sweeney, she brooked being neither patronized nor idealized because of her gender. Nearly every time I brought a date over to meet Ib, the young woman seemed much too soft next to that small, bony, penetrating lady.

Except for the married woman. She came from a family that was on a very early sailing from England in the seventeenth century. "Nothing will come of this," Ib told me, "because you don't want her, let alone her two children, to leave their home and move in with you. And she doesn't want to go, though you both tell each other quite the opposite."

I had come to know the married woman through a jazz program I had by then on WMEX. She started writing in for Bessie Smith records, particularly "Careless Love." Her notes got longer. She wrote like Pat talked, making swift connections between spheres that to squares would seem to have nothing in common. The stationery said "Mrs.," so I just kept the notes to fantasize by. I conjured up a hip intellectual who looked and sounded like Margaret Sullavan. What's the point of fantasizing if you can't get the very best?

Just before the start of a Sunday-afternoon jam session at the Savoy, a slightly husky voice behind me said, "Does 'Careless Love' mean anything to you?" I turned around. There was a woman in her mid-twenties, slender, blond, with the face of a well-bred rebel. She looked like — well, Margaret Sullavan; but she knew my name. At last, the shiksa of my dreams.

To this the bar mitzvah boy had come. Fortunately, the Savoy Café was not one of the places Rabbi Joseph Soloveitchik frequented.

When the married woman wasn't at the Savoy, I paid attention to obsessions other than my own. Sidney Bechet often played the club, and he demanded that his music be taken seriously. Not that he ever said so, but you could tell he wasn't there to blend into the background. The way he stomped off the beat, the way he looked at any sideman who was reserving his energy, and the way he played that long, straight soprano saxophone. The huge Bechet sound, throbbing, slashing the air, as he hurled his band out of themselves and into his control. Nobody, on or off the stand, messed with Sidney Bechet.

One night in 1945, Steve Connolly, wiping the bar, told some of us that Bechet would be coming the next week with a ghost horn, Bunk Johnson. Born in New Orleans in 1879 of a black father and a Black Creek Indian mother,

Bunk had actually played with the fabled Buddy Bolden, whose horn, according to some folks who had been there, could bring people in from miles around. Bunk had not been heard of for many years until he was resurrected by jazz historians Frederic Ramsey, Jr., and Charles Edward Smith. All the time in between had gone into less risky work than jazz — truck driving, working on fairgrounds.

During those years, Bunk Johnson had lost his teeth, but Sidney Bechet's dentist brother in New Orleans had outfitted him with a new set, and he had started playing again.

The first couple of nights at the Savoy, Bunk Johnson, although his tone wavered, gently complemented Bechet with spare, warm, singing lines. But by the end of the week, Bunk had been persistently lionized by college students who had read newspaper stories about this jazz Lazarus. They plied him with booze, then plied him again. By the fourth night, the way Bunk sounded, it would have been a mercy, as one of the regulars put it, if he'd misplaced his teeth.

During the second number of the second set on that fourth night, Sidney Bechet left the bandstand and sat at a table directly below the other musicians. Ordering sixteen cognacs, all at once, Bechet, as soon as he finished one of them, took the empty shot glass and aimed it at Bunk. Some of the glasses missed, some of them hit his shoulders, and a few grazed the side of the trumpet player's head. Bechet would never aim at a musician's lips — or chops, as they were known.

Bravely, soggily, Bunk finished out the set. For the rest of the engagement, he confined his drinking to between the time the Savoy closed and the rising of the sun.

Even more intense than Bechet, and much more voluble, was Jonathan "Jo" Jones, who long ago, on the road, started to be called "the man who plays like the wind." He was not so much a drummer as an orchestra of jazz time. Not only could Jo keep the beat flowing with more élan and wit than anyone else in jazz, but he was also a continuing source of subtly astonishing textures, colors, and rhythmic and melodic designs. As a very young man he had been a dancer, and seated behind the Basie band or any other group, Jo still danced. His wrists, his feet, and his eyes. Especially his eyes — which could also go right through you, if he was displeased with something you had done.

On occasion, when he felt like challenging the notion that a postgraduate jazz drummer required an array of equipment, Jo would leave the bass drums, the high hat, and the rest of his kit. And with just his hands, starting on a chair on the bandstand, he'd take his listeners out of ordinary time into his own universe where he was on such good terms with all of time that it would do just about anything he asked it to.

Moving off the bandstand, playing with his fingers or with the palms of his hands or his knuckles, he drew rhythms and melodies from tables, chairs, the floor, the walls, the very air. Grinning fiercely, Jo kept his listeners, including those who never before could abide a drum solo, ensorceled for as long as an hour. But that was an hour as measured in straight time. To the listeners, that kind of time had stopped; they were in his time.

Having satisfied himself that he had conquered all expectations (except his own), Jo, looking just as crisp as when he had begun, would return to the bandstand and seat himself behind the drums, greatly resembling the Cheshire Cat on the verge of disappearing again.

Jo considered teaching an inescapable responsibility for a jazz musician. Through the years he would select certain "kiddies," as he called them — young musicians, as well as young writers about the music — and instruct them in what, after all, was a spiritual as well as visceral vocation.

"You are a musician," Jo would tell a fledgling horn player. "Do not ever forget that. You can do what very few others can. You can reach people. But to move them, you have to be open to yourself. And you have to be in condition to play everything you hear inside you."

I never found out why Jo tapped me as a candidate for his relentless attention. It happened when I was nineteen. Jo, seated in a back booth at the Savoy, beckoned imperiously. "It is time," he said in his raspy staccato voice, "for you to find out what you have to know if you are going to write about this music."

Jo told me where the music had come from, where he had come from, and how to listen. He leaned forward. "Now, when you hear a jazz musician up on that stand, he is telling you what happened to him this afternoon, the night before, what has happened to him during his whole life. This is serious business. And" — Jo shot me with a long finger — "there is no way a jazz musician, if he is a real jazz musician, can hide any of that, because we play ourselves, not Beethoven or whoever. There is no way a jazz musician can hide whatever he's feeling. He might try. He might put on a big smile and say, 'Man, ain't life grand!' But soon as he starts playing, you can hear the hurt. You understand?

Saxophonist Lester Young, the most intriguing and elusive of the jazz musicians I knew. Courtesy of UMKC special collections

Bandleader Duke Ellington, who talked to me as if I were worth talking to, even though I was as green as grass. Courtesy of UMKC special collections

Trumpeter Rex Stewart, one of the jazz musicians who became my itinerant foster fathers. Courtesy of UMKC special collections

Clarinetist Artie Shaw, whose recording of "Nightmare" was the first jazz I heard, a fierce wailing of brass and reeds, a surging, pulsing cry of yearning that made me cry out too. Courtesy of UMKC special collections

"Okay, now, that gets to the audience. They can't hide, either. A jazz musician gets to them with what he's saying because it's real. So it's not only us musicians who take risks when we play. Depending on how we feel on a given night, the audience is going to go out all smiling or they're going to leave the club way down. And being that far down could be disastrous for some people when they get home. But there's nothing we can do about it, and there's nothing they can do about it."

Seemingly pleased at the egalitarian nature of the danger in jazz, Jo paused, sipped a cognac, and went on. "To be able to play this music, to be able to reach deep into people, that is a God-given privilege. There shouldn't be any debauchery attached to it, either in the musicians or in people who write about it."

"What do I do when I find debauchery?" I asked.

"You tell it to me," said Jo.

From that night on, every once in a while Jo, when he saw me on the street or in a club, would decide it was time for me to be administered another session of instruction while his eyes swept the street or the club like a searchlight. He'd tell me which young musicians I should on no account miss hearing. Some of the names I had never heard of. And he would tell me which of the new ones — and the old ones, for that matter — he was straightening out. Players who had fallen into the debauchery of drugs or booze or bad company. But they could be regenerated, because they had to be — the music could not afford to lose them. I was to watch after them, too.

Jo often spoke of Baby Lovett, a Kansas City drummer of flawless skills. Count Basie had once said of Lovett,

"There's a man that if a fly jumped down on a piece of paper, he'd play it." From all reports, Lovett's character was also without flaw. He helped younger musicians, even before they could get themselves together enough to ask for help; and he was a delight to have on a session even before he got his drums set up. Baby had been married for a long, long time, and when his wife died, he just about stopped functioning. Baby Lovett just sat at home and grieved.

When Jo Jones heard what was happening, he canceled all his engagements for a month, flew to Kansas City, moved in with Baby Lovett, slept in the same bed with him, and, after a time, brought Baby Lovett back to life. It was all part of being a musician, Jo told me later. Anybody who thought there was anything unusual about it just didn't know what the music is about.

Jo Jones often talked about Kansas City, where, in the early 1930s, the music never stopped. There was so much continually swinging music, he told me once, that people would go from one club to another, walking *in time*. Jazz time.

Those of us who came out onto Massachusetts Avenue from the Savoy Café to find our various ways home occasionally walked in jazz time. But it was hard to sustain that pulse and good feeling in the heavy air of Boston, with its tribal hatreds, the anti-Catholics sometimes being almost as venomous as the anti-Semites and all mocking the Negroes — which is why they loved listening to "Amos and Andy" on the radio.

But behind the closed doors of the Savoy, I felt more at home than anywhere else I had ever been, including home. I could not get enough of the music, the deep warmth and the surprise of it. And I could not get enough of the musicians. They were so unlike all the other adults I had known — my father and my uncles; the masters at Boston Latin School; Samuel Caploe, the mighty engine of Sunday's Candies; my professors at Northeastern. I had hardly known those adults. Including my father. I knew him better than the others, of course, but we had never talked about loneliness, failure, women, death, and such things.

The jazzmen, many of them, talked to me with remarkable openness. Remarkable in my life up to then, and since. After hours, for instance, Rex Stewart or Ben Webster, both alumni of Duke Ellington's band, would tell me about their growing-up years, their first experiences with women, their disappointments, some of the rages and griefs they still could not rid themselves of, and the great good bursting times they had known.

Even Ellington, usually the most silken and remote of patricians, once he got used to seeing me around the band, would talk to me as if I were worth talking to, even though I was as green as grass. Mostly he talked to me about his music, how he composed with each musician in the band particularly in mind. "You keep their weaknesses in your head as you write," he said, "and that way you astonish them with their strengths." But he also had advice on keeping a woman interested. ("Nobody likes to be owned. Wanted, yes, but not owned. And that way, of course, you're not limited to just one at a time.")

And once in a while, Ellington would talk about Jim Crow and the abiding delight he'd had in traveling through the South from 1934 to 1936 with two Pullman cars and a seventy-foot baggage car. "We commanded respect. We parked those cars in each railroad station and we lived in them. We had our own water, food, electricity, and sanitary facilities."

Duke smiled. "The natives would come by and they would say, 'What on earth is that?' And we would say, 'That's the way the President travels.' That was in the thirties." Duke looked at me. "You do the very best you can with what you've got."

Years later, I asked some of the musicians I'd known in my teens why they had taken time with me, why they had decided to be my occasional mentors. "That's the way *we* came up," Ben Webster said. "I can't think of a jazz player who didn't have an older musician telling him what he was doing wrong with his horn, what kind of shoes to get, what kind of women he shouldn't mess around with. It comes natural."

Ben was as gentle as his ballad playing. He was a big, yearning man who did change alarmingly, however, when he drank a lot. His nickname among the players was "The Brute." When I was about twenty, I was with him one night in a dreary bar down the street from the Savoy. Ben got into an argument with a stranger, something about cars and engines, and the stranger was a few seconds away from being pounded into the floor when Ben stayed his huge hand and growled at me, "No, I better save this for the horn."

They were all originals, these improvisers. Some less compellingly original than others, but every one of them strode through the world as if he were one of its designers. It was continually astonishing to me as a kid to get to know so many adults who wore no man's collar. Including whatever leader they were playing for. If a sideman felt he was being denied respect, he might not be back for the next set or the next night.

They were also independent in another, not entirely voluntary, way. Sometimes a sideman or even a leader would finish a gig at the Savoy and have nothing else in hand. Work would turn up in time, but I found it frightening to watch this chronic uncertainty. Every adult I knew had some kind of regular job. Even my father, though he was a traveling salesman working largely on commissions, had a circuit of stores in New England he visited regularly. But to not know where you'd be working the next month, or, worse yet, the next week, must be unbearable, I thought. Especially when, as was the case with many of the jazzmen, you're married and have kids.

I'd ask them how they dealt with such regular insecurity, and they found the question odd. That's the way the business was. Sooner or later the phone rang. What else was there to say? I didn't understand the matter-of-fact tone of that answer until I'd worked as a freelance writer for a good many years.

Of the jazzmen I watched in those years, the most intriguing and elusive was a tenor saxophonist who used to say: "In my mind, the way I play, I try not to be a repeater pencil. You dig? I'm always loose in space, lying out there somewhere."

His name was Lester Young, and of all the soloists in the history of jazz, he was the most inventive, influential, and profoundly playful. The first time I saw him off stand, Lester (or "Prez," as everyone called him) was walking alone down Massachusetts Avenue wearing a long black coat that touched the ground and a porkpie hat over his quite long hair (longer than that of any male jazz musician I had ever seen before). And he had an effeminate gait and hand gestures, though he was not a homosexual.

Prez had come onto the jazz scene at a time when Coleman Hawkins's explosive, room-filling sound was the measure by which all other jazz tenors were judged. Young's sound was much lighter, softer, more given to irony than to swagger.

Prez never forgot that when he replaced Coleman Hawkins in Fletcher Henderson's band in 1934 — Hawkins had gone to Europe — "the whole band was buzzing on me. I was rooming at Henderson's house, and Leora Henderson would wake me early in the morning and take me down to the basement and play Hawkins's records for me so I could play like he did. I had in mind what *I* wanted to play, and I was going to play that way, but I just listened to her. I didn't want to hurt her feelings."

Young never could play *big*. As his great good friend of many years Billie Holiday (who first named him Prez) later jubilantly recalled:

"Everyone, when he first started, thought: This man, his *tone* is too *thin*, you know? A tenor sax! Everybody thinks it has to be real big; and Lester used to go out of his mind getting reeds [so he could] sound like Chu Berry [another big-sounding tenor]. And I told Lester, 'It doesn't *matter* because,' I said, 'you have a *beautiful* tone and you *watch*. After a while *everybody's* going to be *copying* you.' And it came to be."

While I was still in Boston, I never talked much to Prez. He was shy, and I was awed. I listened to his music through many nights as he kept going his own gently insistent, insinuatingly lyrical way. I knew from other musicians that his chief companions were gin and marijuana, and I also knew something of the effects on him of his Army experience in the 1940s when a white major from Louisiana found a photograph of Prez's wife, who was white, in Prez's locker. Also found were marijuana and barbiturates. As a consequence, Prez served nine months at hard labor in the detention barracks at Camp Gordon, Georgia.

When he came out of the Army, Prez was more withdrawn, more wary. Yet every night, he picked up his horn and told new tales of romance where it was always springtime. With swinging wit and tenderness, Prez, loose in space, transformed his life every night into what it ought to be. Only serious music is capable of the transformation that is art, the masters at Boston Latin School used to tell me. But it never occurred to them that serious art could come out of a tenor saxophone. Let alone out of a musician with a porkpie hat who said:

"Soft eyes for me. I can't stand no loud shit, you dig? And the bitches come in a place in New York and them trumpets would be screaming, and shit, the bitches put their fingers in their ears, you know. It's got to be sweetness, man, you dig? Sweetness can be funky, filthy, or anything. But which part do you want?"

Looking out the window of Morley's, the musicians' bar — three drinks for what one would cost you next door at the Savoy — I would see Prez, once in a while, flowing along in his long black coat and his porkpie hat. I had the presumptuous notion that I wanted to do something for him, make him feel less alone. I have never seen anyone who was more alone wherever he was. Alone and slightly puzzled. I never could think of anything, except maybe a fifth of gin, but there was nothing distinctive about that. He wouldn't remember me for that.

Years later, though he didn't know it, I helped get Prez a gig on a television show. It turned out to mean more to him than a shipload of gin. The late Robert Herridge, an exuberantly uncompromising television producer-director, wanted to put together a jazz hour on CBS-TV in 1957. Along with Whitney Balliett of *The New Yorker,* I helped select the musicians for the program, among them Billie Holiday and Lester Young.

For a long time the lives of Prez and Lady Day (as he had named her when they were young) had been in as close counterpoint as their sounds on the recordings they made together. But something had shattered the relationship. No one else knew what had gone wrong, including those hipsters who always knew everything that happened behind closed doors.

During the rehearsals for Herridge's "The Sound of Jazz," Lady Day paid no attention to Prez. He was so weak, in any case, that he paid attention to no one. When he wasn't on call, he sat in a corner, in his black porkpie hat and long black coat. At his side was a soft black leather case for his horn. On the set, sitting between Coleman Hawkins and Ben Webster, Prez was willing to do whatever was asked of him, but the booze, the pot, and his distaste for eating had left him with little ability to do what he wanted to do. Eventually, we split his solos between Hawkins and Webster. The only solo Prez had left was in a small combo set with Billie Holiday. The program was shot live, so we had to take a chance that Prez would somehow be able to play at least one chorus in one of the songs.

That song was one of the few blues in Billie's repertoire, her own "Fine and Mellow." On this Sunday afternoon, Lady Day sat on a high stool. Opposite her, in a semicircle, were the players — among them Prez, slumped in a chair. I was in the darkened control room, watching multiple images of Billie and the musicians as the performance began. That afternoon, Lady was singing a blues of triumph. A string of small triumphs really, the triumphs of a survivor. Hell, as much as she'd been through, including prison, she looked good, and she knew that. You could tell she did by the way she had walked through the orchestra at the top of the show. There'd been bad times for Billie, everybody knew that, probably worse times ahead, but look at Lady now. Listen to Lady now. That's what she was singing.

It was time for Prez. Herridge had signaled the floor manager to tell Prez to play from his chair. If he got up, he might collapse on prime time. But when the moment came, Prez stood and, looking at Lady, played in one chorus — its colors those of twilight in October — the sparest, most penetrating blues I have ever heard. Billie, a slight smile on her face, kept nodding to the beat, her eyes meeting Prez's, her nod invoking memories only she and Prez shared. As he ended his solo, Lady's face was full of light and love, and Prez, briefly, was back in the world.

In the control room, Herridge, the associate producer, the engineers, and I were not surprised to see each other crying.

On the set after the hour was over, Billie, pleased with the show, came over and kissed me. Lester was gone, somewhere in space.

Growing up in the jazz world, I learned certain other things that would carry me through this world. And not only from musicians. In Boston, there was a writer on jazz named George Frazier.

He came into a room like the first notes of a Lester Young solo — a proclamation of being, a style that could be mistaken for no one else's. Like Prez when he was not performing, Frazier was a lonely man. He could pour with the best of them, but waiting for the sunrise, he poured for himself.

Out in the world, however, what a grand look to the man! He knew at least as much about tailors and fabrics and the very best buttons as he did about girl singers. (And no one knew more about the sensuous art of distaff jazz vocalizing than George.) Looking contentiously brisk and haughty, George, when he wanted to demonstrate how the exceptionally civilized showed off, might break into Latin, as he did to introduce a concert at the 1958 Newport Jazz Festival one balmy summer day. He did choose to write in English, with a snap that had the sting, and could do much of the damage, of Sugar Ray Robinson's left jab.

George had two primary reasons for writing. First, like all writers, he wanted to call attention to himself. Second, he wanted to call attention to writers, performers, and a very few politicians who had duende. He once explained duende as "heightened panache" or "overpowering presence." At another time he said that while duende is very difficult to define, "when it is there, it is unmistakable, inspiring our awe," making "icy fingers run down our spine."

Lady Day, Lee Wiley, James Michael Curley had duende. "My God," wrote Frazier, "how James Michael Curley had it! How he quickened our memory."

I began reading Frazier in *Down Beat* while I was still going to Latin School, still going to shul—on the High Holidays anyway—in Roxbury. The worlds Frazier wrote about—the elegant Copley Plaza Hotel (did they let Jews in?); the small, very exclusive bars where he would savor the twilight hours; Locke Ober's, where everyone seated on the first floor was a Brahmin, one way or the other—

were as exotic to me as the Saturday morning journeys to the lands of "Let's Pretend" on CBS radio. As enticing and unattainable as those fairy-tale adventures were, so was Frazier's Boston after dark.

But Frazier was not a Brahmin, as I was astonished to discover some years later. Though his bearing made him look as if he might be the direct descendant of William Bradford, Frazier came from South Boston, the son of an Irish Fire Department inspector. He had gone to Harvard, however, and had won the James Bowdoin Writing Prize for an essay on Ernest Hemingway. George would talk about Harvard but not about South Boston. To George, a life should be like a jazz solo—continually regenerated and refashioned, the starting melody long since transmuted in the course of the improvisations.

What compelled me to read Frazier wherever he appeared was his daring. He wrote like Errol Flynn playing Captain Blood. There wasn't the slightest ambiguity about his likes and detestations. Always, he intended to incite his readers, and he succeeded all the writing days of his life. As a Latin School boy, I wrote him indignant letters about his cavalier ridicule of some of the singers I liked. He often wrote back, usually as outrageously as in the comment that caused my letter. But sometimes he was gentler, amused at this tad's capacity for fury.

By this time Frazier was writing the first daily newspaper column in the country on jazz — "Sweet and Lowdown" for the *Boston Herald*. And he had a maddening Saturday morning program on the same station as "Let's Pretend." He would play a series of mystery choruses by three or four saxophonists or trumpeters and not let you know until the end of the program who they were. It was a maddening game because you might be delighted by a particular chorus only to discover that it was a musician you had loudly and persistently claimed could not swing, had a pinched tone, and phrased like a Republican.

(When I went into radio, I adapted — or, rather, stole — George's idea for a weekly classical music hour. I played symphonies and chamber pieces but did not announce the composer, the name of the work, or the identities of the performers until it was over. Through the years, a number of angry listeners complained that I had tricked them into enjoying music they did not like — Tchaikovsky, Grieg, and other "lightweight" composers whose work appealed only to the kind of people who, in a concert hall, clapped at the end of each movement of a work.)

After receiving one of my letters, Frazier invited me to visit him at the *Boston Herald* when I was seventeen. I had never seen a newsroom before. Watching the purposeful commotion — like a jam session closing an Eddie Condon concert — I envied everyone involved, certainly including the copy boys. But I envied Frazier most of all. To get paid for your opinions, the more controversial the better, must be the best of all possible jobs. Every morning, in all the Boston neighborhoods, throughout New England for that matter, citizens sit down to breakfast and open the paper to applaud you. Or, better yet, to roar at you and spill their coffee all over their pants. What a life!

Frazier went on to New York for some years, working for *Life* and then free-lancing. Wherever he was, one of Frazier's abiding pleasures was his enemies list, and by the 1950s I was on it: my ear was tin, my politics were trendy, and my writing style was impenetrable (which was all to the common good, Frazier added).

By the late 1950s Frazier was back in Boston, writing for the *Herald*, and one day there was another line with my name in it. Frazier wrote that through the years I had prostituted myself by writing so many liner notes for jazz albums.

I was living in New York by then; but in my hometown paper, I was on the breakfast tables of New England as the morning tart. The spirit of the First Amendment never came to my mind. And my wife, Margot, strongly suggested, from morn to night, that a man who would not sue upon such outrageous provocation would thereby confirm Frazier's judgment of him.

Through a reporter friend at a paper other than the *Herald*, I retained a vaudeville-like father-and-son team of attorneys. Redheaded, unquenchably feisty, they cannot be blamed for what befell me.

As is the custom in these cases, I, the aggrieved plaintiff, contended that having been called a whore in the pages of a powerful daily paper, I fell apart in mortification. For a lengthy, very lengthy, very dismal period, I was distraught, I could not sleep for nights on end. And when I did slumber, the spirits of countless Hentoffs through the ages, bearded, shaking their heads, pointing, groaned to me in my dreams, "Is this what you have done to our name in America, in front of the goyim?"

Then Margot Hentoff testified in order to corroborate the piteous suffering her good man had endured.

"Tell me, Mrs. Hentoff," said our lawyer, "after he read the reference to him in Mr. Frazier's column, what was your husband's reaction?"

"He was very upset," Mrs. Hentoff answered. "He couldn't sleep."

"Well, how long did this last?" asked our lawyer who had advised her that a year would be an effective answer.

"Well, how long could it last?" the forthright Mrs. Hentoff answered. "Two nights. Three nights."

Much laughter in the courtroom, including the jury box and the bench.

During a recess, the entire legal team of the *Boston Herald* came over to Margot Hentoff. "I want to congratulate you," the senior member said, "on being an honest woman."

The jury decided swiftly for the *Herald* and Frazier. The jury had dutifully listened to my testimony that through the years I had refused offers to do liner notes for music I disliked. But to the jury there was only one germane question. Since my suffering had been so slight, according to so authoritative a witness, why on earth was I wasting everybody's time with this silly lawsuit?

The jury, of course, was right.

To my great good fortune, at the time of my suit against George Frazier, the Boston Strangler was being tried across the river in Cambridge, and the press corps, which would normally have found this trial of some comic interest, paid no attention to it at all.

Even though I remained on his enemies list for several more years, George Frazier never mentioned my dumb libel suit in print. Nor, so far as I know, did he ever mention it in conversation with any of the large number of journalists and musicians we knew in common, for no one ever mentioned it to me.

When we were friends again, I told George one night

that he could have drawn and quartered me in his column, and then some, on the libel suit. Especially after, years later, I had anointed myself an heir of Hugo Black and declared in a number of publications that all libel suits are an offense to the First Amendment. I thanked George for staying his hand.

He was embarrassed, the only time I ever saw George embarrassed, and he waved away my thanks.

In 1974 Frazier, by then a columnist on the *Boston Globe* and still upsetting breakfast tables all over town, found out he had lung cancer. He kept his column going as long as he could, but toward the end, in his hospital room, there wasn't much he could do but read and talk to visitors, particularly his closest friend, Charles Davidson.

"George," Davidson asked during the last week, "are you scared?"

"No, Charlie," said Frazier, "but I'm awfully, awfully sad."

Among those at the *Globe* who were saddest when George died were some of the young reporters and the copy boys. He thought of himself as a mentor, so he talked to them more than most of the other elders on the paper did. And he would tell them his own answer to Duke Ellington's song "What Am I Here For?"

"It's up to me," George would say, "to point out who the bastards really are in this life."

From the first time I read him—in a *Down Beat* concealed in my geography book at Boston Latin School—Frazier was an influence on me. Not his style; that was too calculatedly personal to be adapted by anyone. It was his spirit. His delight in going after the bastards in this life, me among them at one time. His refusal to tone himself down, to be more "balanced," to be "objective," to be "responsible." That was for sidemen in symphony orchestras, not for a horn man in the front line whom people were eager to read because he took chances, because he went outside the chords, because they had no way of knowing what this elegant wild man would do next.

When I was sixteen, those few of my friends who were also deliriously submerged in jazz thought I had gone bonkers when I refused to be in awe of Benny Goodman. I did like the echoes of Yiddishkeit in his phrasing, but they were only echoes. He didn't have the tam, the flavor, of the clarinetists in the Jewish klezmer bands that played weddings at the Aperion Plaza. The rest of Benny Goodman was kind of cold, kind of mechanical, like Dr. Carl S. Ell.

One summer day in 1941, there in *Down Beat* was George Frazier:

> I'm a big boy now and no longer allow myself to be overawed by the big bigness of his name. Benny this and Benny that and the back of me hand to yiz, as I once warned my audience of smart young women! Benny's present band is so damned disappointing that we don't talk about that, my sister and I.
>
> And as for his clarinet playing. . . . Look friends: the greatest clarinet player in the world of jazz is Charles Ellsworth [Pee Wee] Russell. . . . When Benny is dead and gone there will be a lot of men able to follow in his footsteps, but when Pee Wee passes away, there will be no one.

George's writing as writing resounds more for those who used to see it when it first came out than for readers coming to it decades later for the first time. Similarly, I do not think that Frances Sweeney's editorials in the *City Record* on the failure of her Catholic Church to come down on anti-Semitic priests would be enshrined nowadays for the quality of the writing in itself.

But both those Boston Irish lit up the city as long as they were in it, and they put some of their fire in me. And some of their romanticism too.

"The clock," George Frazier wrote at the end of one of his columns, "stands at three and there is honey still for tea."

And later, George, at the crepuscular hour, something stronger, the right brand in the right glass, and Lee Wiley singing.

During my time in Boston, George Frazier seldom came into the Savoy Café. Compared to the Copley Plaza and the Ritz-Carlton, where the fittings were much more suitable to George's station, the Savoy was rather common. But to the regulars, there was no place like it, certainly including home. The music; the conversation; the chance to talk, as if you had been accepted as an equal, with the musicians between sets at Morley's next door. And a regular could watch, over the seasons, love affairs begin, grow, and explode at the Savoy Café. A regular might even become one of the principal players.

One of the evening sports in which the regulars as well

as the musicians occasionally engaged was the "put on." As when two Harvard undergraduates, apprentices in sociology, cased the place for several nights and then decided to compose a thesis about the Savoy. A young woman in her early twenties, Miriam by name, seemed to move with particular ease among the regulars, the musicians, Steve Connolly, and the waitresses. She, the students concluded, would be their informant and guide as they studied the inhabitants of this shadowy subculture.

Miriam's last name was Sargent, and she was another of those descendants of John Winthrop, William Bradford, and that crowd whom I only seemed to be able to meet in jazz clubs. Her father was a Unitarian preacher in rural Maine, so rural that indoor plumbing was seen mainly in catalogues. Her mother, an uncomplaining unpublished poet, was a firm admirer of Sacco and Vanzetti, pointing out that the luminous clarity of their letters was a classic confirmation of the theory that you could find out all you needed to know about someone's character from the quality of his prose.

When she came down from Maine, the hipster provincials in Boston regarded this preacher's wife as too ingenuous for words. But I liked her, because I was fond of Sacco and Vanzetti and fonder still of Mrs. Sargent's daughter, Miriam. The daughter was married at the time to a sometime jazz drummer who also was a sometime cab driver and was taking a long time, as they say, finding himself. Miriam had finished college in Maine and was now waitressing (not at the Savoy) while figuring out whether she wanted to go into the same line of work as psychoanalyst Karen Horney, whom she inordinately admired.

Miriam coolly accepted the offer of the two Harvard undergraduates to be their Vergil; and as she ordered a drink, they asked her to point out, very discreetly, the whores and pimps and drug dealers and confidence men. That she did, transforming the Savoy into a cave of such lurking danger that the two students stopped taking notes for fear of being conspicuous.

The tall, handsome, amiable black bouncer, whose primary avocation was seducing limber college girls with straight blond hair, became a hit man for the Syndicate. A man of principle, he would rub out only whites — except, of course, for tender college girls with straight blond hair. Steve Connolly, at the moment humming "The Wearing of the Green" as he wiped the bar glasses, became a master fence who had sent at least twenty-five once-human packages to Davy Jones's locker in Boston Harbor, because they had tried to cheat this Irish patriot.

And so it went, until Junior Raglin came through the door. Raglin, a very large man, was playing bass at the time with Duke Ellington. Exceptionally kind and gentle, his features were so cast that he looked at times as if he were the enforcer in a particularly unrestrained B movie. Hastily, Miriam informed the Harvard boys in a whisper that the man filling the entire door was her husband. And he was jealous to a lethal fault. Two weeks ago there had been a poor fellow from Framingham, who was only talking to her at the bar, just talking about something George Frazier had written, and he'll never be able to move his left arm again.

Throwing a twenty-dollar bill on the table, the Harvard students thanked Miriam for her aid in their scholarly enterprise and bowed deeply to the bouncer as they went out the door.

We were smug, we nonmusician regulars. Not a black among us. Oh, there were black nonmusician patrons of the Savoy, but somehow they were never part of our crowd. Not really. That did not occur to me then.

Miriam's marriage dissolved soundlessly, and a mutual friend of ours decided to arrange a match between Miriam and me. John Field was a bass player, cab driver, somewhat overly prideful autodidact, and boon companion of the entire Ellington band. Field was so self-involved most of the time that he had no idea how abrasive he was, and so he could not understand why some people disliked him so heartily. But Miriam liked him and so did I, because in looks and attitude he was what I imagined a member of George Washington's Continental Army might have been. Unwilling to accept anybody's yoke, not only that of the British, and sufficiently contentious as to make it a wonder we had kept an army together long enough to defeat the British. Some of Field's ancestors had been in that Continental Army.

Nineteen, I had left home by the time I met John Field. I was living alone in a bohemian part of the Back Bay on a street of New England Conservatory students, jazz musicians, underpaid professors, Pat and Ib, short-story writers searching wanly for epiphanies, robust painters, and other assorted citizens who, whatever their vocations, seemed to enjoy the Ivesian streams of piano, vocal, trumpet, and reed music that came from the windows of the medium-size apartment houses on Hemenway Street.

My mother wanted to know if any of my friends on that street were Jewish. Sure, I said. Were any of the girls on the street Jewish? A few, I said. And the ones I went out with, were they Jewish? I haven't gone out with anybody, Ma, since I moved here. But would you go out with somebody who's not Jewish? Never mind, my mother said, don't answer.

John Field was married to the former Nancy Leahy, who, like most of her sisters and brothers, worked for the telephone company. Nancy apparently had some difficulties, just short of an all-out war, in persuading her family that this summer, good-hearted Catholic girl, as airily beautiful as a melody in a Mozart scherzo, should be allowed to marry a Protestant jazz musician and troublemaker whose income would surely be uncertain until the day he died. And he, more's the pity, had the look of someone who would outlive everybody he knew just to spite them. I found it instructive to hear that not only Jews were unwelcome in certain non-Jewish families.

There was a party one night in the railroad flat of John and Nancy Field. Some of the Savoy regulars, musicians, and a few from the Leahy and Field tribes. Ellington was on the phonograph, and there was much boisterous reminiscing about musicians who had been taken from us because the Lord could never get enough of the good sounds in his own neighborhood—and also because they were terrible lushes.

In a corner, Miriam and I were talking. We talked all night, long after the other guests had wandered off and the Fields had gone to bed. Just before sunrise, we left the apartment and walked along the Fenway, still talking. What about? Ourselves, of course. How we had come to be who we were at that moment; what more we wanted to be and do; how strange that we had never really known each other before; and had there ever been a lovelier morning among the stagnant waters and raggedy trees of the Fenway.

A few nights after our walk on the Fenway, Miriam and I spent a night together. This greenhorn from Roxbury had to be shown what to do.

I was nineteen. I had a girl. I had my own place, and because I was working at the radio station, everybody knew my name. Well, not everybody; but the jazz people — the performers and the laity — knew it, and that was no small thing for a kid just out of the ghetto.

My mother did not share my joy. She could not understand why I would want to leave my family to settle alone in the land of the goyim. Until the very moment I left — the mover's horse and wagon waiting outside on Howland Street — she begged and cried, the only time I'd ever seen her cry. At last, at the door, she put her arms around my neck and, through her tears, said, "Remember, Natie. Never trust a single one of them."

I owed my apartment on Hemenway Street in the Back Bay to jazz. The building was owned by Bernie Moss, an extremely shy, generous, middle-aged bachelor who had found the meaning of life in Sidney Bechet, Duke Ellington, Edmond Hall, Red Allen, and scores more black improvisers. He was often at the Savoy, usually alone, but sometimes with Pat and Ib Patten, who were also his tenants. And he hung out, silently, at a record store near the Savoy. It was there I met him, and soon after, when I was looking for a place in the land of the goyim, he gave me the next vacancy in his building. He took care that none of his tenants ever knew him as a landlord. His brother collected the rent, and the janitor received all the complaints about services. Bernie just showed up to talk about jazz.

It was a tiny apartment. One room and a bathroom, but when I came home there was no one there to ask me where I'd been. No one human. On my first night there, it was evident that I did have companions. In the walls. Remarkably noisy companions. Neither before nor since have I heard such loudly argumentative mice. If they were mice. I was terrified and stayed up all night with the lights on, trying to drive the faceless screeches away with Louis Armstrong's Hot Five and the indomitable Bessie Smith. But after some minutes of silence, the creatures in the walls also had a lot to say about Louis and Bessie.

In the morning, after my first night on Hemenway Street, there was a knock on my door. A soft knock. It was about seven. There was my mother, carrying a tureen of soup. Yes, chicken soup. She knew me, she said. She knew I would never make any soup for myself, because I didn't know how and it would take too much time anyway. And she thought, she said, I might like some nice hot soup in a new place. And I — on my deathbed, this may well be my last memory — I shut the door in her face. Without a word.

I was angry. Here I was, independent at last, and she thought she could find herself a corner in this new life of mine with some soup. If I had shown any sign of yielding, any gratitude, any tenderness, I later told myself, she would become a regular commuter from Roxbury to the Back Bay, carrying gefilte fish and derma and nose drops and rock candy for a sore throat. I had to be firm. I had to show that I wasn't coming home again. Or letting home come to me. That's why I had said nothing. Let her remember only the door in her face.

It worked. She never again came unannounced. And she never brought me any more soup.

Usually, I would have asked Pat for his commentary on the event. But I said nothing to him or to anybody else about the lesson I had taught my mother. I was too ashamed to talk about it. And, of course, she never mentioned it to me.

The squalling mice eventually disappeared. Miriam had also left — for the University of California at Berkeley, where she was determined to get the credits to become at least a psychiatric social worker. The need in the land was great, indeed enormous. Why, just about everyone she knew, very much including me, needed help. That kind of help.

My mother certainly thought so. A few months after I left home, my father called and, rather embarrassed, said he and my mother had been talking, actually *she'd* been doing the talking, and they — she — thought I should see a psychiatrist. It was a simple, basic theory that had been nurtured for centuries among my people. Any Jewish boy who left home before he married had something wrong with him. So my mother wanted to know exactly what had gone wrong inside my head. Do it, my father said, she'll never stop thinking you're crazy unless you see a psychiatrist.

My father did not think I was crazy. He thought I was at sea, but not crazy. What kind of a life was I building, working at a radio station? A college graduate playing jazz records, announcing horse race results and wrestling bouts, reading shampoo and upholstery commercials. What could it lead to? But he expected no answers to such questions from a psychiatrist. All he expected was a bill.

Someone had told my father that the premier psychiatrist in Boston was Dr. Abraham Meyerson, so that's where I was sent. At the session, there was no probing — so far as I could tell — of my childhood traumas, sexual fantasies, or other private matters. The talk was of politics, racism, the verve of James Michael Curley, free speech — the kind of conversation you could pick up at the bar of the Savoy Café.

In due time, my father received a substantial bill — $100, as I remember, which not even lawyers were charging by the hour then — and a professional opinion. I was not crazy. The psychiatrist had found a marked tilt to the left, which Dr. Meyerson assured my parents was not in the least abnormal in young Jewish boys who had gone to college. All in all, nothing was broken, so nothing needed fixing. Dr. Meyerson ended by saying that I was an idealist, a condition that would lead me to certain unpleasant surprises but was otherwise not necessarily a debilitating trait.

"So is Ma satisfied now?" I asked my father.

"It's worse than before," he said. "She thinks Meyerson is a nut and you should go to a real psychiatrist."

had become a radio announcer at the age of nineteen because there was a war on. One afternoon I ran into a fellow alumnus of Sunday's Candies, the Harvard Divinity School scholar, who told me he was now a radio announcer at WMEX and suggested that I call for an audition. I told him I didn't have that kind of voice. He answered that they didn't have all that many voices to choose from because of the draft. Had I had my physical?

As a boy, I had been operated on for a cyst in my left arm. The doctor, a prominent Back Bay physician, was an elderly man with a white beard. He greatly resembled the autumnal Brahms. He did not ordinarily take Jewish patients, but a friend of my father's had intervened. I have no idea whether he was as gruff to his regular patients as he was to my parents and me, but he clearly felt that he was doing us a big favor — against his better judgment — by allowing us to come to his Beacon Street office.

The first time around in the operating room, this distinguished physician absent-mindedly left a small instrument in my arm before stitching it up. Accordingly, a second operation was necessary. And then, because something else had gone awry — he never explained what — I was in surgery for a third time. Consequently, my left arm was now somewhat weaker than my right.

When I went for my physical, I expected — or, rather,

prayed to the God I'd left behind—that the examining doctor, seeing the sad state of that brave left arm, would wave me out of line and stamp me with a 4-F. Instead, the cigar-smoking doctor specializing in arms and legs looked up briefly from his magazine and waved me right along with the other soon-to-be soldiers. I tried to hand him an X-ray and a letter from the famous Brahmin surgeon, but he waved those away, too.

At the end of the line was a doctor who, on adding up the results of the other physicians' appraisals of our various parts, put the fateful stamp of approval or rejection on our papers. I stood before him, stripped of hope that I might be passed over. He looked at a ring on my right hand, and then looked more closely.

"You're a Latin School boy?"

"Yes, sir. And I have this X-ray . . ."

He took the X-ray and the letter and said, "Go back to the doctor who examined your arm. Tell him I want it looked at again."

Heart pounding with the possibility of deliverance, I trotted back to the arms-and-legs man. He snorted. "You can raise the left arm, right?"

"Yes, sir."

"Then I have nothing to change."

Back to the dear, kind doctor who could no longer save me.

"Here," he said, holding out a hand. "I want you to grab my hand with yours, first the right and then the left. And I want you to put all your strength into it."

I gave a mighty squeeze with my right hand. And with my left—well, I rather think there was a little less enthusiasm in that grasp.

The doctor looked at me, looked at my papers, and wrote on the first page "4-F."

And that's how I got into radio.

I wasn't going anywhere at WMEX, as my father, sighing, kept reminding me; on the other hand it seemed to me there were worse things I could have been doing. Advertising, investment banking, white slavery, working for the State Department, corporate law. The list of appalling alternatives was enormous. And at the radio station at least I had my jazz programs, both in the studio and at nightclubs; I was often in the intriguing presence of James Michael Curley; and I had achieved a boyhood dream by getting the best seats in the house at certain sports events. For I was the station's assistant sportscaster.

Frank Fallon, the head of the two-man sports department, was round, gruff, with white hair (and a plaid cap on top of it), and had the sound, rhythms, and phrasing of any patron of a neighborhood bar who was Irish and had always lived in Boston. And that's why he was so popular. There was no side to him, as they used to say. And when you were in his company, if there was any side to you, it began to feel so burdensome that you quickly chucked it away.

I never knew why Frank chose so unlikely a prospect as me to be his assistant. The only sports I had played were baseball-against-the-stairs (with a hard rubber ball) and hit-the-ball in the streets (with the same hard rubber ball). I was a passionate Red Sox fan, but so were hundreds of thousands of other Bostonians. Otherwise, I was so unqualified that I had to take books out of the library on basketball, hockey, and wrestling before each of my first broadcast assignments in those sports. I wanted to get the idioms right at least.

At first my job was to do color. In between rounds or at time-outs, Frank would take a break and I would comment on a particularly amazing play or rattle out the lifetime statistical achievements of the players. Frank also permitted me to have a point of view if I felt strongly enough about something that had happened. "Just be sure of one thing," Fallon told me. "Don't say anything you can't back up." It was, of course, the most useful instruction in journalism I have ever been given.

I appreciated Frank's confidence, but I didn't let it go to my head. For instance, it didn't take long, at ringside and in the fighters' dressing rooms, for me to figure out that some of the boxers were owned by the mob. Men in dark suits to whom I had seen other men in dark suits genuflect in certain nightclubs were granted similar respect, great respect, on fight nights. And some fights came out as queer as a three-dollar bill. Queerer.

I said nothing about any of this on the air. Neither did Frank. We did not believe the peculiar myth that the wise guys never mess with reporters for fear of bad publicity. It struck me that publicity about a disrespectful reporter who had been shot in the mouth would have been just what the men in the dark suits had ordered.

Otherwise, Frank cheerfully collected enemies by denouncing shirking players, managers and owners who were boobs, and fans who threw beer and whiskey bottles at players' heads to demonstrate their manhood.

Frank did feel, however, that we had to give the liveliest possible account of a sports event so as not to disappoint the folks listening in all over New England. After all, they had tuned in with anticipation of a contest, and if we detailed the dreariness we were actually seeing on some nights, we'd spoil *their* night. And they might not tune in again as readily.

So it was one evening with a ten-round boxing bout that had all the tension and danger of a pillow fight among members of Congress. By the seventh round, the crowd was singing a derisive waltz, and singing it quite well, in a sort of open-fields harmony. The lyrics had to do with the gentle pansies in the ring who couldn't bear to be separated from each other.

In the foreground, however, Frank was making each of the desultory blows that landed—when the gladiators weren't hugging each other—into haymakers. To hear him tell it, it was amazing that both fighters had not long since been taken to the emergency room at Massachusetts General Hospital. Meanwhile, the fans' waltz continued, growing in volume and disgust. Frank ignored the choir. And when I took over between rounds, I ignored the choir. When the fight blessedly came to an end, the boos, before a winner was announced, resounded throughout Boston Garden—and, by means of our microphones, all through New England.

Shouting above the boos, Frank told the folks out there that since the bout had been so hard fought all the way, it was understandable that the enthusiastic crowd was expressing its profound disappointment that the fight had to end. By that point, the crowd had been so taken with its own singing that it remained after the verdict was pronounced, roaring out medleys of obscene waltzes at a deserted ring. None of this was reported on WMEX.

Our most memorable collaboration as sports announcers — the fans kept reminding us of it for years — was at one of the annual Knights of Columbus track-and-field meets. To begin with, neither of us was an enthusiast of any contest having to do with track or field. Frank would much rather have seen horses run than humans, and I couldn't get out of my head a similar conviction that such exertions as high jumps and hurdles races were essentially for species that lived that way.

One of this night's major events was a three-mile race. There were a lot of runners, and although they all started at the same place and time, some — on the basis of their records — had been given a half a lap or more advantage over the favorites. At any given point, for instance, a runner may have seemed to be in fifth place but, because of the head start he had been awarded before the race began, that worthy was actually in third place.

Frank and I had all the handicaps written down, but very soon after the runners began to move we were thoroughly confused. In truth, we were distracted before the race began. To begin with, we found ourselves perched over Boston Garden in a steel basket, so small a basket that our engineer, to his great relief, couldn't fit in with us. He had to control the volume from a front-row balcony seat.

Frank and I were so high up that I was mostly focusing on the certainty that if I leaned over a bit too far, my career would truly be at a dead end. Also, before coming to the Garden, in dread of a night full of all those earnest runners and hurdlers, I'd had a few pops (as some of the Irish pols called those shots of sunlight that come from dark bottles). I can't speak for Frank, but he did not usually decline solace in times of imminent adversity.

There was a further difficulty. Frank seemed to have the impression that the management of the Garden had stuck his bulky frame into this puny basket to humiliate him in front of the sports brotherhood, and he occasionally made alarming gestures indicating he was about to climb out and punch someone in the front office in the nose. Had he climbed out, he would, of course, have flattened at least four fans directly below, let alone his own indignant self.

So the three-mile race was not precisely in the forefront of Frank's consciousness or mine. Gamely, however — for Frank always believed that if you stuck at something long enough, it would sooner or later make sense or die — Frank plunged into a description of the thrilling event before us. I, trying to match the chart in front of me with the deceptive order of the runners on the track, kept indicating to him who was really in front and who was really in tenth place.

At some point, it became horrifyingly clear to both of us that we were lost. We didn't know what the hell was happening on that track. Frank, his face red with embarrassment and with fury at the Garden management, looked as if he were finally about to go over the top of the basket while I, taking over at the mike, simultaneously pounded on his shoulder and pointed as forcefully as I could to the depths below. Truculent, Frank sat down and took the mike back.

The awful moment of judgment had come. The final lap was over. Frank stoutly announced the order of the finish. But his voice was not the only one summing up.

Booming behind us into the mike was the voice of the Garden's public-address announcer with the official results. As was evident to every one of our listeners, from Cambridge to Freeport, Maine, Frank and I had every single runner in the wrong order. As one of us would proclaim — for Frank generously gave me the mike after a while — that Pat Jenkins had finished seventh, the public-address announcer, in a merciless obbligato, would authoritatively award seventh place to Ray Bracket. It was like having Rabbi Soloveitchik singing along with me at my bar mitzvah.

We could either confess wholesale error on the air or ignore the voice of truth on the public-address system. Frank and I knew each other too well to have had to consult on what to do. We did not hesitate. We did not equivocate. We signed off as if the voice behind us had been that of a madman and the decent thing to do was to pretend there had been no voice.

From that night on, whenever Frank or I arrived at a sports event in the city of Boston, the sportswriters on the dailies and quite a few fans as well would stop us and favor us with their imitations of how we had covered the by-now fabled three-mile race. Most of the time, these sportsmen could never finish their impressions, for they would soon break into laughter that threatened to break them in two but unfortunately did not. Frank and I, in any case, maintained a dignified blush throughout their carryings on.

My mother probably heard and was mystified by our celebrated broadcast of the three-mile race, for she was WMEX's most faithful listener, even more so than the horse players, who, after all, didn't stay after dark. My mother, on the other hand, listened to the Irish jigs and reels; the Italian hour; the taxpayers' league (represented by an ancient Scotsman with a largely unintelligible burr); the politicians; the Saturday morning newsboys' variety hour, with a bright and sardonic Congressman John F. Kennedy as an occasional guest; the live country-and-western shows; the recorded country music shows; the live black gospel quartets; and Archbishop Richard Cushing roaring through the novena. So long as I introduced any program, she listened until it ended to hear me close the program.

All these years of ecumenical listening, however, did not in the least affect her most cherished beliefs. When I went home to Roxbury for my weekly visit and dinner, I was told again of the eternal hatred all Christians bear all Jews, especially those Christians who marry one of our kind. "A Jew will get into an argument with his shiksa wife," my mother would say, "and before it is over, she will call him a dirty rotten Jew. And she will mean it!"

It was made unmistakably, ringingly clear that if I were to marry a shiksa, it would be the same as driving a stake through the hearts of my parents. Or, if I wanted to be merciful, I could shoot them on my way to my honeymoon.

When I was twenty-five and married Miriam Fonda Sargent, her parents were there in the office of the justice of the peace. My parents were not there, for they did not recognize the union. I was informed through an intermediary — my fifteen-year-old sister, Janet — that my parents would continue to recognize me but that Miriam was a nonperson in a nonmarriage.

Janet, a bright, sensitive student at Girls' Latin, who later became a poet, editor, and college professor, was my only sibling. I was very fond of her, but since she was ten years younger and I had left home when she was nine, I didn't see much of her, being immersed in the land of jazz. I welcomed her good offices in this domestic dispute.

As for their son marrying out of the faith, my parents' attitude was benign compared with that of truly Orthodox parents. In those families, a child who marries a non-Jew is considered to have died, and the family sits in mourning for him — sits shiva. Or so it was in my shtetl.

I told my sister that if they would not receive Miriam at their home, they could start sitting shiva for me immediately. Their response, through the messenger, was that the original offer stood. I could come home anytime. Alone. There was no further communication between me and my parents for several months. I was convinced that my mother was the one who had drawn the bright line. My father, after all, was a man of the world, or at least New England and occasional selling trips to the South. But she — she lived in a shtetl in her head where the dead came in dreams to give signs and alarms, including news of imminent pogroms.

I did not see my parents again until my father had a heart attack and I went to see him in the hospital. The attack had been far from mild. He was under sedation when I saw him, and my mother, materializing behind me, told me, of course, that I had caused my father's heart attack just as surely as if I had battered his heart with my fists.

It was not his first heart attack, and he still smoked three packs of cigarettes a day. Watching him, motionless and far away, I was very frightened, but I told my mother that I accepted no blame for his heart attack. She, I added, by pushing him to cut himself off from his son, might start figuring out her share of the pressures that finally broke him.

She told me the original offer still stood, and if I cared at all for my father, I would accept.

I wished she had a bowl of chicken soup so that I could push it in her face.

A few weeks later, my father, recovering, called and asked if we had furnished our apartment yet. We had some of the customary appointments of those bohemian days — fruit crates transformed into tables, wine bottles become lamps. But we had no furniture in the sense my father meant. Would we like to pick out a sofa and two armchairs?

When would Miriam be coming to dinner?

Anytime she liked.

It was a very comfortable living room set. I was sorry to sell it when our marriage broke up and I eventually went off to New York.

The marriage lasted eight months, and the only clear memory I have of it is its end. In the years before, Miriam and I had always had more to say to each other than there was time. Even when she was in California, getting her undergraduate degree, we spoke in long letters and long phone conversations. But marriage brought silence.

We did work different shifts. I was one of the night announcers at WMEX, and Miriam worked days as an attendant at a state hospital for the insane. But we weren't apart all the time, and yet we were. There were no arguments, just a continually growing distance. And for all of her fascination with, and training in, the psychodynamics of "relationships," we never talked about ours.

One night, she met me at Storeyville, a jazz club off Kenmore Square. I had had a broadcast to do, and when I got off the air and we were having a drink, Miriam said, "I bought a plane ticket."

"Back to California?"

"Yup. Time to get my graduate degree. You can get the divorce here, if you like. You can say," she smiled, "that I hit you. Repeatedly."

I nodded. Although this was the first I'd heard of her leaving and of the divorce, I didn't try to talk her out of it. I had a very clear sense that it would be like trying to convince the wind to blow in another direction.

When we got home, I moved out of the bedroom into the living room. I was very civilized.

The night before she was to leave, I suddenly had an uncontrollable urge to sleep with her. Well, almost uncontrollable. Miriam said that if I touched her again, she would call the cops. I hadn't the slightest doubt that she would. In the morning, we said good-bye gently and quickly.

In the divorce court, I told the judge that Miriam had thrown coffee cups at me. Repeatedly.

After the divorce, my parents had the grace to keep religion out of it.

Years later, when I had come to New York and was married for the second time (that one lasted five years and resulted in two daughters), Miriam and I met in a coffee shop. She was in briefly from California, where she was a psychiatric social worker and a union organizer among her colleagues. I rode with her to the airport. We held hands all the way, not saying much. The distance between us had disappeared. We kidded each other about my going all the way to California with her. Kidding on the square, as they used to say.

On the way home, I felt that I had been unfaithful to my second wife. And I didn't feel a bit guilty.

Over the years, some members of Duke Ellington's band would ask me whatever had happened to Candy, as Duke's men called her, and I'd tell them. And they'd say Candy always had class. Which was true.

After my marriage to Miriam evaporated, I spent all my nights at the jazz clubs. One of these was Storeyville, run by a stocky, determined young pianist, George Wein, who was eventually to reveal formidable skills as a worldwide jazz entrepreneur.

In 1952, Wein brought the Dave Brubeck Quartet to his club for the first time. The craggy Brubeck looked like the kind of guileless, humorless minister who, with his bright eye and crushing handshake, could send certain souls straight to the devil in desperate need of relief from shadeless virtue. And Brubeck played the piano as if he were happily clearing a lifelong trail through a forest of giant sequoias. He took an axe to the beat and therefore did not swing.

As Brubeck played, his alto saxophonist Paul Desmond, leaned against the piano, hands folded over his horn. Bemused, Desmond seemed to be in a state of reverie amid the hearty clangor — an amiable solitary at the revival meeting.

Then, long-legged, lean, slightly stooped, Desmond would approach the microphone and transform the night. With a mesmeric purity of tone, Desmond spun cool, sensuous melodic variations on the theme of the moment. Although Brubeck was still fighting Indians in the background, Paul drew the audience into another, much gentler private fantasy. Romantic, but not sentimental. He was all too aware of how close yearning is to feeling ridiculous. And he would never embarrass his admirers by sounding as vulnerable as he actually felt. Indeed, after an especially lyrical solo, Desmond would grin. Nothing lasts, the grin would say, not even longing.

In addition to his silvery melodic lines, Desmond was one of the wittiest of improvisers. His ear was extraordinarily quick and true; his mind made eerily apposite connections. He would take a phrase that someone had played earlier or summon a tipsy fragment from Stravinsky or someone else not present and seed it into his solo. Paul would build on that fugitive air with judicious irony and elegance until we were quite turned inside out.

Desmond and I became close friends. We talked for hours about women, writing, movies (he "discovered" Ingmar Bergman and a number of other European filmmakers before I'd heard of them), death, bad marriages, loneliness, and women. We were both in love with Audrey Hepburn, not that we ever informed that finespun lady of our intentions. I had never before had a friend who seemed, in so large a sense, to be me.

At one point, I came upon a conflict between friendship and what might be called integrity. I was reviewing recordings for *Down Beat* at the time, after I had left Boston, and in those years a negative review in that journal could mightily injure sales, and feelings. A new album by Desmond was dismayingly flawed, I thought, by arrangements crafted of sugar and niceness. I could have praised the album anyway, noting a reservation or two very briefly. Or I could say what I thought. After all, Paul was worldly, maybe the most worldly of all jazz musicians. He was aware of the ethical imperatives of critics, and therefore he was most unlikely to let an honest, if cutting, review affect so deep and long-lasting a friendship.

I decided to say what I thought. The friendship ended. But I followed his work through various musicians, and I found out that he kept up with mine as well. It had been years since I saw him when, one night at a club in Greenwich Village, there was Paul, sitting near the bar, the grin the same. But he looked tired. We talked with great gusto, exchanged phone numbers, and promised to keep in touch, in real touch.

Not long after, he was dead. Cancer. Three packs a day. In his last months, a club owner, Bradley Cunningham, used to spend some time at Paul's apartment to see to his needs. "Paul would leave the door open," Bradley said. "He was so weak he figured that if he needed help, people should be able to get in without any trouble."

One morning, Charles Mingus, the formidably spontaneous bassist, composer, and leader, decided to visit Desmond and cheer him up. (Mingus did not know that it had been many, many years since Paul had awakened before three in the afternoon.) This was a morning on which Mingus felt like cutting a bold swath through the world. And so he came uptown in a black Spanish cowboy hat and a heavy, swirling, black cape.

In through the door strode this grave, imposing figure. Desmond, his eyes opening, struggled to focus on the apparition and then, sorting through his memory, found the compelling chess-playing harvester of us all in *The Seventh Seal.*

"Okay," Desmond said to Bradley Cunningham, who was standing near his bed, "set up the chessboard." And grinned.

According to the obituary in the *New York Times,* Paul Desmond left no immediate survivors.

A few weeks after Paul's death, in the summer of 1977, some of his friends met at a Columbia Records studio in New York. Paul's music played softly. There were a few short speeches and stories about him, all low-key, some very funny. The piano had been tuned, but nobody had played. Then, from the back of the room, Jimmy Rowles, wiry, graying, wearing a golf hat and a quizzical look not unlike Paul's, moved almost at a run to the piano and said, "This is a song Paul always asked for."

Jimmy Rowles played "Darn That Dream," fitting it to

Paul's tone, floating beat, and grin. Done, Jimmy got up, danced a small jig, and uttered a cry. Not in mourning. It was what Thomas Wolfe, the one whose mother ran a boarding house, called a goat cry. To life. To Paul's music.

The album I gave only a couple of stars to years before wasn't all that bad, come to think about it, as I often do.

I had first gotten to know Paul Desmond because of the nightly broadcasts I did from Storeyville. I also had a jazz record program on the station, and Paul was a guest. So were Duke Ellington, Sidney Bechet, Frankie Newton, Rex Stewart, and scores more of my boyhood heroes. And they were still my heroes, even though I had come to actually know them and their frailties.

Of all the interviews, the one I remember most clearly was a session with Sandy Williams, a gnarled trombonist who had worked with Fletcher Henderson, Chick Webb, Coleman Hawkins, and Rex Stewart, among other major leaguers. Sandy still had his distinctively warm, boisterous sound, but he had begun to run out of exuberance before the end of a solo. He was tired.

Sandy Williams had brought with him to the studio a shy, attractive woman in her late twenties who listened to everything he said with devoted concentration. During the program, while a record was playing, Williams pointed to the huge, round clock on the wall. It was a standard studio clock with a red sweep second hand. "You keep your eyes on that second hand," Sandy Williams told his companion. "Just keep your eyes on it. Every second that goes by, that's one second less you have in your life."

For the rest of the program, she never took her eyes off that clock. And when the half-hour was over, it was with great reluctance that she left that clock, her lifeline.

For the rest of the night, and for a good many nights thereafter, I watched the clock for her.

Although the jazz programs attracted a steady, if not a large audience, and although I was a pretty good utility infielder (sports, news, politics), WMEX's portly chief executive officer, William Poté, did not like me. Indeed, he greatly disliked me.

For one thing, Mr. Poté was convinced I was a Communist. Most of the guests on my programs were black. I never wore a tie, and day in, day out, I wore a black leather jacket. That told him something. Also, he saw me shamelessly reading something called *Partisan Review,* and I had interviewed Pete Seeger on the air without denouncing his un-Americanism. What more proof did he need?

When I pointed out to the boss that I had been for Norman Thomas in the 1948 presidential campaign and not for Henry Wallace, Mr. Poté was not in the least reassured. He knew what Norman Thomas was. Then I added that at the last minute I had switched to Harry Truman. "So you say." Mr. Poté glared at me.

He particularly disliked me because I had helped convince the other announcers to join AFRA (American Federation of Radio Artists — a "T" has since been added). Poté had never dreamed he would live to see his announcers organized, as if they were coal miners. No more split shifts — working four hours in the morning and another four at night. The end of a salary scale that made it very hazardous for any announcer to marry unless his wife worked. And the creation of a cruel break in the extended family at the station now that this alien presence, the union, had been brought in. And who had brought in this dark presence? Comrade Hentoff.

Before the union won the election to become our bargaining agent, the boss, with enormous pleasure, was about to fire me, but his lawyer told him that he would quite probably be charged with an unfair labor practice since I was one of the organizers. After the union came in, Poté desperately wanted to fire me, but if he tried, the union lawyers would make his life even more miserable because my forced exit would have a chilling effect in other shops AFRA was trying to organize.

There came a time, however, when I made William Poté the happiest of men. He and several other officials of the station were deeply involved on that day in one of the poker games that flourished in the spacious executive offices. Fortunately for the solvency of WMEX, there were sales representatives and a station manager who actually worked while the high-level card games went on. It was well known that the poker tourney was never to be interrupted unless the station was on fire, the Russians had landed and were nearing Kenmore Square, or the Red Sox at Fenway Park next door had won the pennant. Nonetheless, I came into the gaming room one afternoon in November in complete confidence that my information would more than justify the disruption of the game.

I told Mr. Poté that I had been awarded a Fulbright fellowship for study in Paris and would like to request a one-year leave.

Poté pumped my hand as he instantly agreed to the leave. Under no condition, he said, was I to hurry my studies. Knowing me, the boss said, he was sure I would love Paris and maybe want to stay there for a few years — twenty or thirty, maybe. "A party!" he roared at the station officials. "We must have a gala, a truly gala going-away party for this young man who has made us all so proud."

Whatever "gala" means, the party was large and expensive. With tears in his smiling eyes, the boss gave me a set of luggage and once more assured me that my job would be safe — for a hundred years.

My grant was to have begun in February. But this was the first year of the Fulbright fellowships, and there had been delays in the starting times for some of the countries involved because not all the paperwork had been correlated. In January I received a letter telling me that on reflection, it had been decided that I would begin my studies in Paris in September. Starting in February would lead to too many fiscal and scheduling difficulties. The letter ended with the hope that I had not been unduly inconvenienced.

Inconvenienced? Not at all. In two weeks I would be getting my last paycheck from WMEX. I had already been given my gala going-away party by the station, and the Savoy regulars had also bade me a long and boisterous farewell. Why, everybody I knew had already put me out of mind.

I had two choices. I could wait until the fall to take my Fulbright, meanwhile slinking back to WMEX and the

Savoy with a disgustingly sheepish grin. Actually, that was the only reasonable choice I had. My Government had spoken. The passage money would not come until August. My living expenses—in the currency of the country where I'd be staying—would not be available until September. What could I do but sidle back, to the snickers of my colleagues at the station and the smoldering frustration of my boss, who would probably want the luggage back.

The only reasonable choice was intolerable. I told no one about the change in dates. I borrowed money from my father to book passage on a liner leaving from New York in three weeks. As friends and shopkeepers kept bidding me farewell, I smiled right back, my throat closing in panic.

Arriving in Paris with not much more than an open-ended return boat ticket, I went straight to the office in the American Embassy where the Fulbright fellowships were administered.

A young functionary with a slight Southern drawl and the air of a son of property looked at me with a pronounced lack of enthusiasm. It was impossible. There was no place for me in the budget. I was a September person. That had all been made clear to me in the letter. Did I think that by just showing up and taking a bow, I would be rewarded for having crossed the Atlantic on speculation?

Well, yes, I said. I'd had to believe that, and I explained the dismal alternative if I had stayed home.

The functionary shook his head. There is simply no place for you, he said. Since I had no place to go, except back to the Atlantic Ocean, I stayed. And argued.

No, he kept shaking his head. No room. No room.

As an American citizen and an admirer of William Fulbright, who surely had not intended a winner of one of his grants to suffer miserably as a result, I insisted on seeing this apparatchik's superior. Said superior was a long-term State Department officer who appeared bemused as he heard my story.

"Quite a few other people," he said, "must have been greatly inconvenienced by the change in dates. But they didn't go rushing off to Paris." He paused. "More's the pity for them."

When I left his office, the superior told me to ask the young apparatchik to come inside. After about ten minutes the Southerner, faintly disdainful, returned to his desk and gave me various forms to fill out, the name and address of a bank where I would receive my monthly funds, and a final shake of the head.

"Very irregular," he said. "Really."

I could keep the awful luggage.

In my application for the Fulbright, I had written of my intention to research and write a comparative study of T. S. Eliot and Paul Valéry. Working in radio had given me a lot of time to read — much more variously than I had in college — and I actually intended to do that study.

Both writers had been in such passionate need of formal restrictions, Eliot insisting that "poetry is an escape from emotion," as his rhythms mocked his denial. And Valéry, much more conscious of the metaphysical intimations in everything he did and everything he hid, seemed to me the very embodiment of pure thought (paradox intended). Or as close to pure thought as anyone who wrote so sensuously, so musically, had come in this century. I wanted to contrast Eliot, who required religious faith to deepen his intellect, and Valéry, who kept finding more than enough mystery in his own acutely subtle mind.

I never wrote a line of that paper. There was too much else to do. Cinéclubs, book stalls, plays, cafés, trips to castles in the north and trips to castles in the south. And the jazz *caves*.

At one of them, Sidney Bechet was working with a young group of French "traditionalists" who had learned how to play what they thought was jazz through memorizing old recordings, including the scratches. Some of those recordings had been by Sidney Bechet. I watched him as, with his cold eye, he looked at these French boys pretending to be black men who had grown old. Pretending to be Sidney Bechet, for God's sake. But Bechet had never forgotten that you could not freeze this music, you could not hold it. You had to move with it. And pounding out the beat, sending a blast of life through his long, straight horn, like the shofar on Rosh Hashanah, Bechet lifted these young Frenchmen as if he were a typhoon and hurled them into the music. He left no time, no room, for them to remember the licks they had stolen. They either had to find something of their own to play or perish in the storm.

I was supposed to be taking courses in French poetry, among other things, at the Sorbonne, but I went only when it was too cold in my one room with the bathroom down the hall. Unlike most other Fulbright students I met, I was not concerned with getting academic credits to enrich an academic career back home. I had no such career, nor did I want one, so it didn't matter whether I went to class or not.

Some years before, it would have mattered to me. Even at Latin School, where I was a feckless scholar — once making a deal with a physics teacher whereby I received an F for the year in return for the freedom to read whatever I liked during class — I expected somehow to become a professor. A lifetime of respect and long summers; economic security beyond the vagaries of commerce; a preserve where no one raised his voice and where at twilight, without fail, a glass of sherry would appear. With maybe a small piece of pickled herring. I was determined not to forget my roots.

During my first year at Northeastern, while I still felt my life was destroyed because of where I'd wound up, I wildly applied to Harvard for a transfer. At the end of that first year, Harvard said to come ahead, with a full scholarship, but I decided to stay where I was — with the *Northeastern News* and with my new friends in the student body who were actual working parts of the real world.

I still figured, though, that my true vocation was a tenured position somewhere; and in my last year at Northeastern I had applied for — and been awarded — a fellowship at Harvard for study toward a newly established doctoral degree in American studies. I began with a paper on Phillis Wheatley, the child brought to Boston from Africa as a slave who became a much-respected American poet (except by Jefferson, who thought she was being patronized). I fully intended, however, to do my final work — a historic breakthrough in the academy — establishing Duke

Ellington as the preeminent extension of what F. O. Matthiessen had called the "American Renaissance."

I never wrote a line of that paper, either. Not at Harvard, anyway. I didn't stay long enough. By the beginning of my second semester in graduate school, I had dropped two courses because I was still working full-time at WMEX. While I had managed to cram for "American Constitutional Law" during the nightly novenas and to do some of the reading for F. O. Matthiessen's American poetry course while sitting next to Frank Fallon during the wrestling matches, I knew, as a blues lyric put it, what a hole I was in, and so let the other courses go.

There was a deeper problem. I was less and less sure why I was at Harvard. One afternoon I was pleasurably lost in the stacks at Widener Library — instead of working on a paper that was due — when a professor with whom I was studying American literature came by. Tall, spare, reserved, with a wit so dry it passed most students by, he had almost become the president of a most distinguished university. But an affair he had been having with the wife of a distinguished colleague made the newspapers, and he knew that forevermore, or until retirement, he would only be lecturing here on Jonathan Edwards, Emerson, Whitman, Twain, and those other fellows whom he knew all too well.

Year after year, however, he was a quietly compelling lecturer. He was too proud not to be. The authority of the man was quite remarkable. Even the few radicals in the class fenced very gingerly with him as they tried, and failed, to find an opening for Marx to turn the New England Transcendentalists on their bourgeois heads. And one morning a very large dog walked into the auditorium as the professor was lecturing before a combined Harvard and Rad-cliffe class. Unhurried, self-assured, the dog proceeded down the center aisle and stopped directly in front of the professor. "Wrong class," he said matter-of-factly and continued his rather skeptical analysis of an Emily Dickinson poem as the dog, with an aplomb equal to the lecturer's, turned around and walked slowly back up the aisle and out the door.

I'm not sure why that scene always comes so readily and satisfyingly to my mind. Something to do, I suppose, with the indivisibility of true civility.

That afternoon, in the stacks of Widener, the professor of American literature surprised me by knowing my name. It was a big class, and he mostly lectured, seldom calling on anybody.

"Tell me," he said, "why are you here? I mean in the Ph.D. program?"

I planned to teach. I planned to teach American studies.

"I listen to you on the radio," he said. "The jazz pro-gram, some of the other things. My sense is that out there" — he gestured in the general direction of Boston — "is where you ought to be. I think you might find it too confining among us, as the years go on. Well, it came to mind when I saw you. You might think about it."

He started walking away, stopped, turned around, and said, "No reflection on your work, you understand, al-though I do think you try too hard to make a case for Phillis Wheatley the poet. The case for Phillis herself is clear. An admirable survivor. But would you be as enthralled with her verses if she were white?"

A week or so later, on a Sunday night, I was in the read-ing room at Widener, doing research for a paper the same professor had assigned. It had to do with James Fenimore Cooper and the extent to which he had actually known any Indians. Looking at the books stacked in front of me, I realized, as soon as I really thought about it, that I had no real interest in James Fenimore Cooper. So what on earth was I doing there?

I brought the books back to the main desk and left the library. It was early enough to catch Sidney Bechet's last two sets at the Savoy Café. The next morning I took a leave of absence from Harvard Graduate School. I am still on leave.

And that's why, in Paris, I wrote no papers and took no exams at the Sorbonne.

In Paris, I was free to do as I liked all day and all night long. One of the things I chose to do — my mother would have been astonished had she known — was to have a Jewish dinner every Friday night at the home of a family, the Sorkines, whose daughter, Fenya, I had known when she was an exchange student in Boston.

The father had been in a concentration camp. One night he told me that many of the men with whom he had been shipped to the camp had been killed soon after their arrival. How had he survived?

"The Nazis asked for volunteers to build something," he told me, puffing on his pipe. "Most of the others, wanting to ingratiate themselves with these animals, stepped forward. I figured this was a way the Nazis amused themselves, so I stayed where I was. Those who volunteered were, of course, not seen again."

It was a warm, contentious, self-assured, generous family, and all of them, from the kids still in school to the parents, seemed thoroughly sure of their places in French life.

"Of course," the father said to me as I was leaving one night, "you can never trust them completely."

I did not have to ask whom he meant, Mother.

My job at WMEX was still open when I came back. "Whatsa matter, you didn't like Paris?" the boss, near tears, greeted me.

Nothing else had changed much. I ended each night at some jazz club. The married woman, who had moved away with her husband and children, came back for a time, and we told each other that we couldn't bear being apart again. But she wouldn't leave her husband, and I didn't want her to.

I still lived on Hemenway Street and walked to work every afternoon through the Fenway. And every afternoon I would tell myself that I had walked this route so often through the years that I knew practically every bush and brackish bit of water, every drooping tree, and exactly how many steps it took to get from my stairs to the place where I was to start the workday by broadcasting the race results.

And every day, as a punishment for all my sins — starting with the eating of a salami sandwich in plain view on Yom Kippur — I asked myself: "Is this what the rest of your life is going to be?"

Would I ever get to the big time?

I had heard Coleman Hawkins talk about the big time: "New York makes *all* musicians sound kind of funny when they come around. When they first come here, I don't care what they were in their hometowns, when they come *here*, they get cut. They get cut every time. They have to come here and learn all over again, practically. . . . New York . . . I have never seen it fail."

Would I get cut in New York? If I did, could I learn all over again? Would I get to New York to find out if I could make it in the big time?

I had started a column for *Down Beat* that was sufficiently quarrelsome and arrogant to bring a good deal of mail, the tenor of which suggested that I set my face to the Atlantic Ocean and keep walking in that direction.

Pleased at the reader interest, the publisher of *Down Beat* asked me if I wanted to become New York editor of the Musicians' Bible, as it was called then. He mentioned that the salary would be $175. Since the magazine came out every two weeks, I assumed he meant that I would be paid $175 every two weeks. I'd sure have to scrimp, but I wasn't going to turn down a chance at the big time over a salary dispute.

After I got to New York, it was a relief, when my salary checks for $175 began arriving weekly.

William S. Poté didn't give me a farewell party this time. He was sure I'd turn up again. My mother was sure I wouldn't and was very sad.

I was kind of sad too. I walked around a lot the day I was offered the New York job at *Down Beat*.

In Roxbury, there were more blacks on the edges of my neighborhood. The herring man was gone, but inside the Blue Hill Avenue synagogue near his old stand, burning old men dissected a line in the Talmud while a dark sparrow of a soon-to-be bar mitzvah boy watched.

I remembered some of those old men, from D-Day on, grabbing the first edition of the *Daily Record* at dark, hurrying back inside Segal's Cafeteria, and checking to see how many Jewish names were in the list of the dead. God forbid there were none that day so it looked as if the Jews were not doing their part in the war against Hitler.

At the Aperion Plaza, the kitchen was busy preparing for a wedding, but no one was in the room used for a synagogue. I sat down near where my father davened on the High Holidays, and I heard not the chazzan but the decidedly nonreligious klezmorim, whose sounds used to bring me running down the block when I was five. The klezmorim, the itinerant improvisers without whom any wedding would be a funeral.

Getting up, I walked to the vantage point on the sidewalk where I used to be able to look through the Aperion Plaza fence and see the klezmorim. The strutting trumpet player, bending and cracking his notes like he was eating nuts, winking at the bride and at any other girl up to ninety. The clarinetist, my hero, his notes dancing, making even the rebbe nod with a little smile, and playing with such a cry, a krechts, in his clarinet whenever a song brought back all that Jews had gone through to be able to drink and dance in this place in America.

My father would come to find me staring through the fence, and I would beg to stay for one more song, two more songs.

When I was older, in my teens, I would still come running as I heard, a block away, the klezmorim and their musical cartwheels. The melodies like sun showers, the rhythms that should have been bottled like seltzer water. There was nothing else like it. Except jazz.

"So," the klezmer clarinetist would say to me, "where do you think Benny Goodman came from?"

I didn't bring up Pee Wee Russell or Edmond Hall. I just enjoyed.

That afternoon of wandering around the city I was about to leave, I would have gone anywhere in Boston to hear a klezmer band, but there was no bulletin board. So I walked crosstown to peer into the window of the Savoy. I have never gotten used to the look of a nightclub in daylight, chairs on the tables, ghosts on the bandstand. That afternoon I saw the shade of Oran "Hot Lips" Page as, a year before, on a stormy night, he had been singing the blues for an hour, a whole hour, in that rough, sweet voice. It was like an unabridged oral history of centuries of blues. "I didn't repeat myself, did I?" he said later. "Hell, I could have gone on for a week."

I saw, longer ago, Miriam glaring at the married woman across the room, but none of that would ever matter again.

And I heard, in a back booth, Jo Jones remembering Kansas City: "There was a black tailor downtown who'd take our measurements uptown and then bring the clothes back up. It was a great city for music, but blacks couldn't buy clothes downtown."

Back at the radio station, Frank Fallon was getting his evening script together. Good-byes terrified him because he might get corny. "Remember, kid," Frank said, "if you've got the goods on them, there's nothing they can do to you. Except kill you."

I walked across the Fenway, and it was then I felt like shouting. Being a Boston Jewish boy, I did not. But I was listening to the driving beat and leaping horns of Muggsy Spanier's Ragtime Band — the vinegary Rod Cless on clarinet; the blustery, ass-pinching trombone of George Brunies; and the Irish walloper, Muggsy, who got that name — Kid Muggs, actually — from Louis Armstrong, when Muggsy was fourteen in Chicago and Louis was his rebbe.

And I heard George Brunies pounding out the words, just the way he played that trombone:

> I wished I could shimmy like my sister Kate,
> Now she shakes like jelly on a plate. . . .
> Every boy in my neighborhood
> Knew she could shimmy, and it's understood,
> I may be late
> But I'll be up to date
> When I can shimmy like my sister Kate —
> I'm shoutin' —
> Shimmy like my sister Kate!
> Oh, boy.

At the "Oh, boy," I did a jig I had seen Frank Fallon's long, tall niece, Mary Trank, do. And I bowed, like Frances Sweeney.

George Frazier had been thirty-one when he first left for New York, where he discovered what he already knew: "Boston may be great, but New York — New York is the varsity."

I was twenty-eight. George had come back to Boston. I was not going to. No matter what. After all, did the herring man go back to the old country?

But I couldn't move on yet. I had to get clearance to leave from the state legislature's Committee to Curb Communism. I had not been subpoenaed, but I had an unnerving hunch that if I didn't check in before I left Boston, I could well be dragged back from New York once they got to my name on their list.

This was 1953, a year before Joseph McCarthy was unequivocally condemned by the United States Senate — more for dishonoring that body than the Bill of Rights. But in 1953, Massachusetts, like many other states, was still officially and eagerly hunting for Reds. The Commonwealth's Committee to Curb Communism had been holding public hearings at the State House in Boston for several years. The witnesses before the committee were treated with full presumption of guilt, and anyone taking the Fifth Amendment was addressed as if the tumbril had just arrived to transport him to the guillotine.

The chairman of the committee, Senator Philip Bowker of Brookline, was an honest man, conservative in all things, and wholly convinced that subversives were gnawing away at the foundation of the Commonwealth at an alarming rate.

In its 1951 report, the Committee to Curb Communism had warned any Red who thought he or she could hide behind the skirts of the Constitution that "our constitutional liberties are not defenseless before those who would subvert and destroy them, any more than freedom of speech affords a right to subvert and destroy our government. The Bill of Rights is not a suicide pact."

What did I have to fear from the committee? I could recite passages from *Darkness at Noon* by heart. I had publicly and quite nastily attacked supporters of Henry Wallace's 1948 presidential campaign as Comsymps. And at a tender age, I had resisted being recruited into the Young Communist League by my barber. But there had been a time when I had indeed appeared to cross the Red line, and I knew that the record of this transgression must be in many hands.

As I was to find out twenty-one years later, when I received my FBI dossier through the Freedom of Information Act, J. Edgar Hoover's legions did indeed know what I had done. There I was, the "subject" of an investigation characterized as a "security matter." The probe had begun in the late 1940s because I had been listed in the catalogue of the Samuel Adams School for Social Studies three years before as a teacher of "the story of jazz."

The Samuel Adams School, my investigator—name inked out—had noted, "has been declared to be an adjunct of the Communist Party by the Attorney General of the United States."

It had been quite clear to me when I was teaching there that the directors of the school regarded the Soviet Union with affection and unlimited trust. That was obvious from some of the names of the faculty—longtime rationalizers of every turn in the Soviet line—as well of the courses. And it was clangingly obvious when each week, a young woman would stride into my class, as she did into all the classes, to announce the "progressive" round of fund raisers, special lectures, and political action meetings for the forthcoming week. Most of the students for my course had come to the Samuel Adams School only because they had been listening to my jazz programs on WMEX. Among them were Republicans, Democrats, and some Norman Thomas Socialists but no one, I think, who had a picture of Stalin on his night table. Accordingly, they were startled each week by all these calls to join the imminent repeal of bourgeois values and power.

I was at the Samuel Adams School, however, because I was jazz crazy, a jazz missionary. Nobody had ever asked me to teach a course on the music before, and since I had been assured that no one at the school would try to tell me how to teach it, I knowingly, if gingerly, took a place — apart — on the faculty. No one there ever did tell me the politically correct way to speak of Louis Armstrong and Lester Young, but just in case an FBI agent had registered for the course, I occasionally contrasted the indomitable individualism in jazz with the collectively "responsible" house bands of the USSR.

Actually, while teaching at the Samuel Adams School I occasionally fantasized being called before a committee on Un-American Activities — preferably on the national level. I would tell them that although I had every right to refuse to answer their un-American questions on First Amendment grounds — for they had no business inquiring into my political beliefs and associations — I was going to cast aside my constitutional shield. I would answer every one of their questions and shame them for having so ludicrous a Red-hunting apparatus that they had fished up a certified, life-long anti-Communist. And there I would be in the newsreels, triumphantly producing an American flag and scat-singing "When the Saints Go Marching In" as I proudly waved that flag.

By the early 1950s, as the pursuit of Reds intensified in the nation and in the Commonwealth of Massachusetts, my fantasy became somewhat more grim, as it seemed to me that an official inquiry might well be held concerning my evenings at the Samuel Adams School. People had lost their jobs for less suspicious activities.

As I told the regulars at the Savoy, I still intended to shame any committee that called me. I would resist their right to summon me, but once subpoenaed, I would crush them with the truth.

When the chance came, however, to go to New York and work for *Down Beat*, my combat plans also changed. I wanted a clean break with Boston. I wasn't going to wait for the Committee to Curb Communism to get to me. I would force its hand. The battle would be joined, and I would be able to leave the City of Boston like a mensch.

But I was also afraid. Who knew what they had in my file? What lies that could take months or years to expose and disinfect? Worst of all, who knew what I might do in my desperate desire not to lose this chance to get to New York? I knew some Communists — public party members. Would I hand over their names in return for being stamped kosher? Of course not. But could I be sure I wouldn't give the names? After all, if I knew they were Communists, the committee must know they were Communists. So what harm would be done? But that was no excuse. To give one single name, even Joseph Stalin, was to legitimize the committee, Joe McCarthy, and all the other despoilers of the Constitution.

I made an appointment to see Senator Bowker. The chairman of the Committee to Curb Communism was soft-spoken, courteous, and, it seemed, confused on the morning I came to see him. He had checked with his staff, the senator told me, and there had been no plans to call me. Had they overlooked something? Was there something I wanted to tell him to clear my conscience?

Not at all. I started to list my credentials as an anti-Communist, starting, of course, with *Darkness at Noon*. The senator had not heard of the book, or of Arthur Koestler, nor did he seem at all interested in anything concerning either one of them or their relationship to me.

The senator looked into a file in front of him, and then he looked at me. "Why did you agree to teach at the Samuel Adams School?" he asked.

"Because it was a chance to teach about jazz."

The senator's eyebrows went up slightly, and I realized he didn't know Lester Young from Jack Benny's Rochester.

"Who else was teaching there while you were teaching?"

"They're all in the catalogue."

"Would you please name those you remember?"

I named a few, starting with F. O. Matthiessen, with whom I'd had a course at Harvard and greatly admired for the passion as well as the quality of his scholarship. "They're all in the catalogue," I said at the end by way of trying to cleanse myself.

Senator Bowker thanked me and said I could go to New York in peace. I was not going to be called before the committee. As I left, he looked at me again in considerable puzzlement, still not sure why I had come.

I left Senator Bowker's office with the unbearable knowledge that I had turned myself into Whittaker Chambers. The challenge of trying to make the varsity in New York had lost its excitement. Whether I made it or not, I would always know, inside, that I had named names. From the catalogue, to be sure, but I had actually come to the senator — voluntarily, not by subpoena — and put myself in the position of being asked for those names. And I had not refused to give those names.

I wanted to talk about what I had done, but I was so ashamed there was no one I could tell. I spent that night and the next at the Savoy, and the regulars took my dourness as a sign that I had already begun to be homesick for the club.

The third night, Stix, a young trumpet player I'd often talked with at the bar, came in after he'd finished work at Izzy Ort's, a club that would have been right at home in Dodge City before there were marshals in the town. He looked about as grim as I did.

"You know where I'm working?" Stix said. "Not out front on the bar but in the back room where it's all closed in for what they call dancing. No windows and just that one door with that gunsel on it. You ever been in there?"

I hadn't. Too much noise to hear the music.

"Yeah. Grunts. Every night, apes banging on those chicks. They're not any hookers that I know, but they're some kind of hookers or they wouldn't take what they take. I start at four in the fucking afternoon and I get through at twelve, and every night that room gets smaller, you know, and I want to yell." Stix laughed. "You know where that would

get me. Black cat screaming in a white man's place of business. Shee-it. They'd throw me in the loony bin forever.
And you know, maybe they'd be right. You ain't looking
all that together yourself."

I told him what I had done. And then I told him something that had just struck me. "Bowker said they were
through with me, but I bet that was just to throw me off.
Now that I've come to them, now that I've called attention
to myself, they're going to see me as a friendly witness,
somebody they can put on the stand, somebody who can
talk about what went on at the school. So what I went
there to do — get a ticket to leave the city without having
to look back — I did just the opposite."

Stix shook his head. "You're going to drive yourself into
a loony bin. They got nothing on you."

"That's dumb!" I yelled, startling the bartender. "Don't
you read the papers?"

"Got no time," Stix said. "I go to school days, remember?"

The Savoy was closing, and we went to an after-hours
joint around the corner. But the music and the drinks were
bad, so about three in the morning, we sat down at the
counter of a back-of-town diner where musicians, waitresses off work, and marginal entrepreneurs hung out.

Just as the bacon and eggs, toast, and French fries came,
the front door was kicked open. Hard. Standing there,
holding a submachine gun, was a short, thin, black man
in his mid-forties. Carefully, he surveyed the room, starting
at the counter and then looking at the faces in the booths.
Without a word, he turned around and left.

Nobody said anything for a while, though a number of
the customers lit cigarettes with a little difficulty. As I asked

for another order of French fries, Stix turned to me and laughed. "Okay, now you got the word. The man just told you you're not wanted here. So move on, damn it, while you can."

I left for New York a few nights later. I never did hear again from the Committee to Curb Communism. However, when I obtained my FBI files in 1979, I saw that the Boston office of the Bureau had sent my dossier to the New York FBI around the time I took the train at South Station. And as my New York dossier grew, there was an entry on June 28, 1967: "Nathan Irving Hentoff/Security Matter . . . On June 4, 1948, a source, who had furnished reliable information in the past, made available information that Hentoff was paid $30.00 for services rendered by him in a teaching capacity at the Samuel Adams School."

After a few weeks in my new city, much of Boston began to seem far away. Except for certain scenes and voices that still refuse to disappear — the herring man, the boy eating the salami sandwich in plain view on Yom Kippur, the chazzan, the assembly hall at Boston Latin School with the centuries-old names carved into the wall, James Michael Curley, the Savoy Café, Miriam, Ben Webster, and especially Frances Sweeney, often laughing at life, and showing us Boston boys the great fun of knowing that we didn't have to bow to anyone so long as we had our facts straight.

I wasn't thinking of Frances Sweeney when I went to see Senator Bowker. If I had let her come to mind, I'd have been too angry at myself to go inside his door. I swore I would not forget her again, having grown up enough, sort of, to leave home knowing that the Boston boy she had started to work on still had a long way to go.

Frances Sweeney went with me, and so did the music, for Bix Beiderbecke was right: "One of the things I like about jazz, kid, is I don't know what's going to happen next. Do you?"